The Nature

and Evolution

of Female Sexuality

Mary Jane Sherfey, M. D.

THE NATURE
AND EVOLUTION
OF FEMALE
SEXUALITY

Random House, New York

Redrawn Diagrams by Charlotte Staub.
"Introduction to Sex Research Project," *by Robert N. Rutherford, M.D.,*
originally appeared in the January-February issue of Western
Journal of Surgery, Obstetrics and Gynecology. *Reprinted by permission*
of author.

Library of Congress Cataloging in Publication Data

Sherfey, Mary Jane, 1933–
The nature and evolution of female sexuality.

Bibliography: p.
1. Sex (Biology) 2. Sex (Psychology)
3. Generative organs, Female. I. Title.
QP259.S53   612.62   69–16458
ISBN 0–394–46539–3
Manufactured in the United States of America by American Book-
Stratford Press, New York, N. Y.
2 3 4 5 6 7 8 9
First Edition

To Dr. William H. Masters
and Virginia Johnson Masters
this book is gratefully dedicated

Knowledge is like a sphere in space; the higher it rises, the more it balloons.

—PASCAL

We regret for ourselves that which we cannot really know. We regret for others that which we cannot really teach them.

—J. ROBERT OPPENHEIMER

PREFACE

On the other hand it should be made quite clear that the uncertainty of our speculation has been greatly increased by the necessity for borrowing from the science of biology. Biology is truly a land of unlimited possibilities. We may expect it to give us the most surprising information and we cannot guess what answers it will return in a few dozen years to the questions we have put to it. They may be of a kind which will blow away the whole of our artificial structure of hypotheses.

—*Sigmund Freud* (*17*)*

The few dozen years have passed and biology is indeed returning to us the most surprising information. This book is a biological study of female sexual evolution and functioning with emphasis on those aspects most relevant to human sexuality, psychoanalytic theory, and Freud's enduring "artificial structure of hypotheses."

Three phenomena of female sexuality are unique (or almost so) to *Homo sapiens* and remain inadequately understood:

* NOTE: Numbers within parentheses are keyed to references in the Sources (pp. 183–188).

the premenstrual tension syndrome; our "silent" ovulation, i.e., the escape from estrus periodicity bringing on our capacity for continuous sexual arousal; and (questionably) the orgasm in women.* I would like to show that these three uniquely human characteristics are related to each other and are the result of the evolution of man from the quadrupedal to the bipedal posture, and with the development of man's other unique characteristics, resulted in the human mating system.

Originally my interest had been in the evolutionary origins of premenstrual tension. It soon became apparent that all three phenomena could be aspects of a unified process, stemming from the profound changes occurring during the prolonged evolution of the female reproductive system— with the orgasm being *perhaps* the final event (thus far) in a long progression of adaptations.

The vital importance of the nature of the orgasm to the psychoanalytic theory of female sexuality urges that special attention be given to the question of this phenomenon.

I have divided this investigation into two parts. Volume I comprises the present work and deals, first, with the nature of bisexuality in the light of the modern inductor theory of primary sexual differentiation; and, secondly, with the demonstration of the nature of the orgasm in women by a presentation of the decisive research of William H. Masters and his collaborators at the Washington University School of Medicine.† Many of the implications of these two series

---

* A probable fourth unique feature of human sexuality is the menopause. Most infrahuman females seem to be fertile until death or very late senility, especially in captivity. However, this feature involves mechanisms not directly concerned with those under consideration and is omitted here.
† The scope and significance of this research have not been sufficiently appreciated, nor has its pervasive meanings for psychoanalytic theory and evolutionary biology been explored. M. Heiman (23, 51) is the only psychoanalyst who has used these findings; however, since he could utilize only the first fragment of the entire data now available, the comprehensive import of the research was not indicated. Moreover, of Heiman's

of recent biological advances for our understanding of the psychosexual development of women will be detailed.

Volume II, to be published, presents the phylogenesis of the female external genitalia, secondary sexual characteristics, and sexual behavior through the primate line of descent. Recent concepts in evolutionary biology and population genetics will clarify the relevance of these fundamental facts to the establishment of the human mating bonds, to the relationship between the sexes, and to the socialization of man. All of which will take us back to—or leads us up to—"civilization and its discontents."

This investigation is the initial product of a fairly global approach to the study of man, requiring familiarity with physiology, anatomy, comparative embryology, endocrinology, gynecology, palaeontology, evolutionary biology, population genetics, primatology, and ethology—not to mention anthropology and psychiatry, the central foci upon which the rest converge. I am well aware of the inordinate hazards in such an undertaking; yet the extreme importance of cutting across the compartmentalization of knowledge makes the sacrifice of accuracy in details, inherent in any such venture, more than compensated for by the expanded vision of man. (Keeping up with the ever-ongoing deluge of current literature is, of course, one of the major difficulties.) By purposively omitting the all-important psychological forces with which psychiatry explicitly deals and limiting this paper to the explication of these recent biological discoveries, some semblance of comprehensiveness is possible. At the same time, many cultural correlations can be readily discerned because of the fact (not commonly realized, I believe) that nothing binds man's genetic code more closely to his culture than his reproductive tract.

---

many interesting physical correlations, the implication that the Masters data support the psychoanalytic theory of female psychosexuality requires certain reconsiderations (see Chapter 3).

From all this biology, I will propose certain theoretical concepts which may or may not be valid. More important, however, is my hope that this study will serve both to further the growing rapprochement between biology and psychiatry and will stand as a basic reference, a biological foundation —to be remodeled as new findings dictate—with which any psychological theory of female sexuality must be integrated.

CONTENTS

The Nature

and Evolution

of Female Sexuality

INTRODUCTION

This is the first book in a two-volume study of the nature and origins of female sexuality, the sexual structures of the female, their behavior, and *her* behavior; and because it is not possible to understand the sexuality of the female without the male, nor the sexuality of both without reference to reproduction, the book includes all three. Volume I concentrates on the nature and meanings of several recent developments in biological and medical research on human sexuality. These developments may have considerable import for psychiatry and medicine as well as for anthropology. They also touch on the relationships between men and women, and on religion and philosophy—especially where the former fades off into mythology and the latter touches the mind-body problem. Volume II will describe the physical and cultural evolution of the sexuality of animals and humans with a focus on the females of the species. In short, Volume I tells how things are; Volume II will tell how they got that way.

Almost three-quarters of the material in each of these two volumes will treat new data and ideas in biology. The other one-quarter is unevenly divided between anthropology and psychiatry, with psychiatry getting the lamb's share. Coming from a psychiatrist, this may seem a strange division of interests, but it is my strong belief that psychiatry, to its detriment, has traditionally paid too little attention to these other fields—and all roads lead to Rome.

The Kinsey Bow-Ties

My introduction to the very odd idea and neglected need for the study of human sexuality as a serious scientific discipline in its own right came about quite naturally. Indiana is that state of the Union which prides itself in the fact that its soil produces almost 99 percent of the country's yearly crop of top-quality grass roots. This special breed of Midwesterner is fond of asserting proudly, "I'm a Hoosier, born and bred!" and, being one myself, my own heritage of Hoosier patriotism led me to Indiana University. Along with all the other pre-medical students, and as many students from other departments as could be jammed into the university's largest lecture hall, I took Dr. Alfred Kinsey's course on sexuality, which the school euphemistically called Marriage. It was one of the first of the Kinsey courses, I believe, given only two or three years after he began his epoch-making, data-gathering interviews, and about ten years before the publication of his first and most famous book on the sexual behavior of the human male.

Sex education was just getting into college curricula; and, Indiana, not to be outdone by the Ivy League, felt obliged to follow suit. It hedged its risk, however, by appointing an authority on wasps from the biology department as the sole teacher of this subject. The utter incongruity of the idea that a man of bugs would be better equipped to teach this subject than a psychologist, psychiatrist, gynecologist, or whatever, apparently did not bother the administration, the faculty, or the students. (I certainly recall no comment from other students, and insofar as I remember, I did not even know that Dr. Kinsey had been an authority on the sexless, parthogenetic gall wasps until his book appeared in 1949 and created an avalanche of praise and scorn.)

Moreover, I do not remember Dr. Kinsey as a fascinating teacher; in fact, I would say that he managed to accomplish what at the time we would have thought impossible: he made a history-making course on sexuality for undergraduate students unbelievably dull. In part, I suppose this was done deliberately, since then (as now) every serious scientist interested in the topic as his chosen lifework had to pretend that it was boring beyond belief—that he was a man totally devoid of humor, that he never could and never would listen to nor tell an off-color joke nor utter a profane word, and that if there was any connection at all between sex and pleasure he had never heard about it. In total, the whole subject was to be treated with all the conviviality of a course in Economic Statistics II, and was in addition, academically insignificant (i.e., our course was one credit, one hour weekly lecture with no roll call, no study assignments, no papers, no examinations, and no grades).

No doubt Dr. Kinsey seemed a good choice to the faculty committee; after all, he had already gathered and classified about 17,000 gall wasps. He and his family had held an impeccable position in Bloomington and in the university's small-town life for seventeen years. He was a shy man who seemed socially ill-at-ease in large gatherings, talked little, avoided the faculty's social life, their fights, their feuds, and their friendships; and he had no enemies.

One can be quite sure, however, that the committee would have never appointed him to teach Indiana University's first course on "marriage" had they known of the dynamic reservoir of energy they would be setting free. No doubt they were smugly satisfied as they acted out their appointed roles in this Greek tragedy (or rather comedy) on the banks of the Wabash far away.

To those of us sitting high above him in the lecture amphitheater, there were signals emanating from the man that soon hinted that once having been given sex as a scientific subject, he would find himself compelled to transform it into a matter of high statistical moment, which for those of us with no numbers in our souls meant a stodgy, banal business.

On first impression, Dr. Kinsey's face seemed too deeply lined for his 45 years and for its near immobility; he rarely smiled at us. Neither face nor voice seemed to reveal an emotional reaction to anything. No students gathered around him after class asking questions. His clear but monotonous Midwestern twang was so distinct and natural that we simply assumed he was a Hoosier, born and bred. (He was from Hoboken!) Dr. Kinsey was, unquestionably, one of the ten worst dressed men of eminence this country has ever produced. His head was covered with flying hair that always seemed as if it had invented a scheme for defying combs. His clothes were almost execrable; nonetheless he invariably wore a little bow-tie. Although bow-ties were more fashionable then than now, they were hardly mandatory; on Dr. Kinsey they looked just plain funny. Yet, there they always were: the faultlessly neat, tiny bow providing a trim dividing line between two sets of shambles, rather like a plumber in a cummerbund. To make matters worse, when I first saw him, he had apparently just had his hair cut—or thought he had—or maybe had bolted from the barber's chair in the middle of the job. Anyway, it looked like a crew-cut half-done, neatly and closely cropped around the back and sides but left much too long in front, where it seemed to stick straight up. Amused and bemused are the only words I can use to describe how this initial unforgettable picture of Alfred Kinsey affected me: the high forehead overseeing the lined, gentle face with its quick, wise eyes inadequately demarcated from the sturdy, masculine body by the silly little bow-tie—and with his hair standing on end, he looked as though he were in a perpetual state of surprise, somewhat like the endearing look of a little boy who has never ceased finding all the world and all the people in it absolutely astonishing.

So there he stood week after week with the dead-pan face and nasal voice twanging monotonously on and on and on. We heard about the mean average frequency of prostitution in Bloomington, Indiana, versus Chicago; and about the percentile differences between the average number and frequency of nocturnal emissions in college-bred and noncollege-bred men with all figures corrected against the total U.S. population according to the 1940 census. We heard about the total average frequency per week of intercourse for married men at all age ranges with figures seasonally adjusted. We pondered over the mean, median, and range for the percentage of orgasms per week in upper-class married and non-married, churchgoing and non-churchgoing Protestant women compared to the same figures for Catholic and Jewish women, with each statistical summary expressed with levels of confidence in the statistical accuracy according to somebody's way of confidently computing accurately leveled statistics. We heard about penile lengths, vaginas, orgasms, coital positions, animal contacts, and homosexual experiences—all described numerically in that same deadly monotone. I left Dr. Kinsey's class at the end of the first few lectures with the vague feeling that he must be trying to tell us that sex was (or if not, should be) performed under a wet blanket—it could be a colorful one, but it must be wet.

When the course ended, I could not remember a single statistic the man had so laboriously gathered for us; and I felt as if I had learned but two Hard Facts (the things he kept telling us we were there to learn). The first one was that if one heard a forbidden word, like penis or orgasm, spoken frequently and matter-of-factly it soon lost absolutely all its shock value; the second Hard Fact I learned was that there sure was an awful lot of sex going on.

Why did I not drop such a meaningless, no-credit course? Or at least cut most of the sessions? I think that the thought never occurred to me; nor, I guess, did it to the other students—there was rarely an empty seat in the large lecture hall. Why in later years did I always put Dr. Kinsey's name at the top of the list of the best college teachers I had; and yet be unable to explain why? Why did those bow-ties continue to fascinate me? Each week I carefully examined each one as best I could from the distance (he wore some, I swear, that were made of plastic—to obviate dry-cleaning, I suppose); I kept waiting to see him in a real flashy one. I never did. Everyone knew Kinsey by his bow-ties; they were his trademark. Yet trademarks, like profane words, cease to attract attention when seen frequently. I realized that those ties had meanings for me they did not hold for others. But what were they?

Before the course was half over, I think I knew, and the others knew, that here was a man many times greater than the sum of all the parts we had heard about him. Here was a man who in some mysterious way could communicate something about the mystery of sex while he was lecturing about numerical frequencies. I do not know how he did it.

Kinsey was the first scientist I ever heard of who openly confessed his faults and mistakes, especially those made while interviewing people. He did not want us to repeat them. It really mattered to him that he had hurt the feelings of a middle-aged spinster from Peoria, that an old lady from Indianapolis had gotten up and left in the middle of her interview, that the shy student who had started talking freely about himself ended by telling lies about his sex life. As he related these things, one felt the compassion that Kinsey felt for these people he believed he had wronged.

The other characteristic of the man that came to us between his words was his incorruptibility. He had told the faculty committee which appointed him exactly what he intended to do with the job. That they did not believe one man could interview 10,000 people by himself was their problem. If he could have no assistants, he would do it alone Kinsey was never a man to work in groups; he did not need or want such support. He was a loner and did not want others to pull or push him away from the path he believed was the right one. Later on, we read that with the publication of his first book fame and fortune had come to him— and had had no effect: he just went right on as before, interviewing more and more people. I doubt that anyone who knew the man was surprised.

One day near the end of the term I had just come from a philosophy class in which the professor had held forth at length on Descartes and the mind-body dichotomy. While crossing the campus, I had a flash of insight about the bow-ties that was to satisfy me for many years. It is the neck that separates the head (mind) from the body (sex). How a man decorates his neck may tell much about the way he relates those two parts of himself. The neck is nothing, a swiveling link, conveniently located for ties. A conventional tie means a conventional mind-body relationship, that is, a dichotomy. A bow-tie, especially if worn constantly, not as a fad, meant an unconventional relationship. Suddenly Kinsey's mind and body seemed on very close and intimate terms with each other with only that fragile little tie, a toy holding them apart. (I might add that this conclusion made me feel quite pleased with myself and, of course, with Dr. Kinsey.)

One final note, a personal one, on Dr. Kinsey's bow-ties that needs but to be told to speak volumes. My years of medical school and psychiatric training passed; and other than the fact that any memory of those undergraduate years would cause the image of Kinsey to float briefly before my mind, I thought little of him. In 1949 my father died. A few weeks later and back in New York City, I dreamed the most vivid dream I can remember having dreamt before or since. I was walking through a lovely very dark forest and came upon a beautiful clearing magically aglow—rather like those we so frequently see on Christmas cards, with the crèche scene in the center of the clearing surrounded by kneeling rabbits, wolves, and deer. But there was no crèche in my dream clearing. It was empty. As I stood at the edge, a giant oak tree snapped at its base and crashed thunderously to the ground. I watched horrified as it fell; but when the ground stopped shaking and the trees quivering I got up on the trunk, which was now as wide and long as a redwood. I had taken hardly two steps along it when I noticed that the rough bark was moving, rearranging its patterns, until before me was the figure of my father lying dead, peaceful and quiet, in his coffin. The oak bark faithfully formed the face of the man and the exact clothing he wore in his casket except for one detail: he had on that which he had never owned, a neat little bow-tie.

The Premenstrual Tension Story

I was interested in the menses and the premenstrual tension syndrome almost since I can remember, and wanted to do research on the problem. However, such research was not being done anyplace I went—few men evinced the slightest interest in this medical problem—and in the large hospitals, one does what everyone else is doing, which is usually what the head of the department is doing. Not until I began full-time private practice could I work on this subject. Within a few months I was deep in the subject of the evolution of female sexuality.

Freud discerned that the first strong emotional reaction to a person or thing that a child associates with sexual arousal will remain with him as a sexually stimulating person or thing. I have come to believe that something on the same order occurs with the first menses. No matter how much a little girl is prepared intellectually for the menses, the first intensely emotional reactions she experiences associated with them will remain with her throughout life. Contrary to sexual arousal, with the menses the experiences are all too frequently unpleasant or painful; and almost always carry some note of ostracism, or taboo. (I cannot yet prove this theory with anything near Kinsey's standards for proof; but at least I am sure it does occur in a large number of girls.) The following example is the one with which I am most familiar.

My own menses started at age twelve; my discomfort was mild compared to that of many of my friends—with whom one could only sympathize and commiserate. On the second day of that first period I had it from my highest authority on these matters, my second-best girlfriend, whose uncle was a doctor in St. Louis, that the menstrual flow was really the remains of a dead baby. If you had sex, the baby was fertilized and you got pregnant; if not, the baby died and the menses were all that remained of it. I did not doubt this explanation. I began asking questions however, about how come we are the way we are. Most questions were ultimately answered simply: "God made us that way." The more I thought about it, the sadder I got. All those dead babies! It seemed so cruel and even more so that I had to catch the few remains of my own baby month after month on an absorbent napkin and flush him down the toilet. I also decided that there was something wrong about God's attitude towards women. After all, He created the baby in me, in the first place, and He must realize that I was forbidden to have sex and fertilize the baby until I was married (or much older). So He made the baby and then murdered it—all inside me! Not only did He murder the baby He ground him all up until he was just blood and stuff. I felt an immense sense of pity for the little bits of baby that were coming out of me. Moreover I did not like the attitude of other girls about it. To be sick was all right; but to call it the "curse" and make dirty jokes about it now seemed inhuman. I vowed then and there that I would not be that way, and that I would do something about it. I started making plans for my next period.

When it arrived twenty-eight days later, I was ready with a large shoe box which I had carefully painted brown with some old paint I had found around the house and saved for this purpose, and a large mass of white wrapping paper I had retrieved from the Christmas decorations stored in the attic. As each napkin became stained, I carefully wrapped it in its Christmas-paper shroud and laid it in the shoe box, which I hid at the back of my closet. Five days and some fifteen napkins later, I had the complete mortal remains of my baby laid in his little coffin. (My first baby was to be a boy, naturally. We had not heard about Women's Lib and such then.) When no one was around, I carried the coffin tied with a white ribbon to the garden. Under the large apple tree and behind the garage where it would not be noticed, I had dug the grave and now with a splendid feeling of solemn awe, I laid my baby in his grave and spaded the earth over him. Then I stood beside the tiny grave and said aloud the 23rd Psalm and the Lord's Prayer. With a whispered "Good-bye, little baby!" the funeral service was over. I was content.

During the next month, so many people told me I was wrong about the menses being an unfertilized dead baby that I gave up my resolution to treat my menses with all the respect and mourning that death demanded. The alternative explanations were never very satisfactory. I did not know that the same year that I conducted my first and only funeral service, the endocrinologists were beginning to ask the right questions and get some of the right answers about the menses. All the right answers are still not yet in.

Nor did I realize that the idea that the menses were the macerated remains of an unfertilized baby had been the accepted explanation by almost all of mankind until less than a hundred years ago. It was the logical conclusion on the basis of the easily observable facts of women's reproductive cycles. I know of no ancient or illiterate societies that reacted to this conclusion in the same way I did. But I was a child of the twentieth century, from which the Devil, the Evil Spirits, Black Magic, and angry gods to appease had disappeared. My one God was benevolent and, I was beginning to think, pretty stupid, at least as an Architect designing nests for women's eggs.

The Long Road to Publication

After many delays caused by all the usual things that delay beginnings, not the least of which was my fascination with psychiatry, I left the psychiatric clinic where I had previously practiced full time and was finally free to research any subject I wished—free, that is, as much as one can be with a full-time private practice. I went straight to the premenstrual problem and then floundered about for over two years trying to find the footholds in the mountain where one person could climb. (Ironically, one of my main purposes in going into private practice—I could choose my own patients—became one of my major stumbling blocks. I had hoped to be treating five or six patients with premenstrual tension at all times. Almost all women had or had had it; but I do not recall ever having a patient who came to psychotherapy for that reason. Even those who suffered quite severely were not interested in finding out why, especially since I had no new remedies to offer. In about fifteen years of practice, I managed to treat fairly intensively twenty-one women whose premenstrual tension was a major, although secondary, problem.)

After reading all the medical literature, I finally was forced to accept the obvious with all its implications of hard work. The tension was but a symptom of the menses, and no one really knew why we had the menses, why they were necessary, how they had evolved. I had to go back to the origins, study evolution, and, because only the primate female menstruates, study the monkeys. This led me to the subjects of ethology (behavior) and to sexuality in general where much work was being done with an occasional detail about the menses thrown in. In 1961 I discovered the inductor theory—the theory that the mammalian male is derived from the female and not the other way around—and at the same time found that studies based on this theory had been hanging about the literature for the past ten years attracting no attention. Nobody, save the few research endocrinologists who developed the theory, had ever heard of it. I could only assume that this finding, which to me was a breathtaking, history-making discovery of the first magnitude with implications for everyone, had been ignored unconsciously because both the men who had made the discovery and those who had read the duly recorded data did not *want* this fact to be true. From that point on, I knew what I had to do: I had to bring this startling revelation to the attention of psychiatrists in such a way that they could not ignore it. To my mind, this meant that first I had to bring this fact to the attention of the psychoanalysts because the Freudians had always been the chief theorists of psychiatry and because this embryological fact would strike a body blow at the Freudian concepts of female sexual development, one of the few original theories of Freud that have remained unchanged since he wrote about them.

But first I had to be sure of my scientific material—I was wading in unfamiliar waters, and there was still an unanswered problem that stuck like a painful thorn in my side. Women's sexual response was tied to the vagina not only by Freud's theory, but by everyday observation, by commonsense. Yet nowhere in the evolutionary studies could I find any evidence for how the vaginal orgasm came to be. The evolution of the clitoral mechanism was clear and unquestionable; yet I could find no more physical reason for how a vaginal orgasm came about in the most primitive monkeys, or any other animals, than in women. This was a crucial point, I thought, for if the inductor theory was right, then one had to explain why, if the vagina developed first, it then acted like a new structure, or an old one with a new function imposed upon it, so new that only women had it or so new that it could only operate after a long and proper psychological conditioning during childhood. All organs are subject to psychic influences, but none like this, none that requires psychic influences in childhood in order to operate at all. The inductor theory and Freud's vaginal orgasm seemed to confront each other like diametrically opposed mutually exclusive ideas. One or the other was wrong.

I spent a year reading masses of embryological, genetic, and endocrinological data trying to find the necessary confirmation of my extension of the inductor theory and increasingly became disconsolate about the whole idea. Then within one-half hour on a Saturday afternoon in 1962 I found what I wanted by pure chance. I had gone to my most frequented haunt, the New York Academy of Medicine Library, which is second only to the Library of Congress in its collection of medical and biological journals and books, to look up some unpromising references. Among them was one whose title and contents I have forgotten; its only value lay in the fact that it was in a 1960 issue of *The Western Journal of Obstetrics, Gynecology, and Surgery* (a fine journal but one that I doubt many psychiatrists have ever laid eyes on). Flipping through the pages to my references, I stopped briefly to note the lead article, and then my eyes fell upon the editor's preface and remained glued there. The preface in itself was unheard-of in medical journalism, at least to my knowledge. I reproduce it here both as a brief document of historic dimensions and because its very oddity induced me to read the article it introduced.

Introducing the Sex Research Project:

Nearly six years ago, the Sex Research Project was established within the framework of the Department of Obstetrics and Gynecology at Washington University School of Medicine at St. Louis. It is with considerable professional pride that the Western Journal presents the following paper by Dr. W. H. Masters. This is the first of a series of studies on the anatomic behavior of the human female vagina during its sexual response. The "Kinsey-Group" has brought to relatively complete fruition the interview technic for acquiring information regarding the human male and female sex responses. The Sex Research Project was developed to explore the basic physiology, of which no precise and substantial knowledge has been collected scientifically to date.

This group's approach follows the dictum of Dr. Carl Hartman—that it is not the province of research to explain everything. It is, rather, the duty of duly constituted research effort to collect the facts. Once sufficient basic knowledge is available, the paths of resolution for major problems usually become relatively obvious. With this first presentation, which we regard editorially and scientifically as fulfilling these criteria, Dr. Masters reports the first basic anatomic study.

Other similar studies will, step-by-step, develop the

constellation of physiologic interrelationships in this relatively unknown area. These studies will be presented in future issues in a fashion similar to this first paper. We feel that this is most significant material being collected in a completely acceptable and scientific fashion.

Robert N. Rutherford, M.D.
Editor

Here was an editor of a medical journal beyond reproach telling his readers that it was all right to read the following article; it was not pornographic. It was of course the first of the Masters and Johnson articles to see the light of print.

I read this first Masters and Johnson article as fast as I could. I knew it was a major breakthrough in the study of human sexuality. Then I ripped through all subsequent journals to see if more articles had appeared. I found the second one, and in the last issue just put on the shelf, found the third, the study of the clitoris. It was truly a Eureka-experience for me. This was it! Freud was wrong. Men were wrong. Women were wrong. Common sense was wrong. There was no such thing as the vaginal orgasm as heretofore conceived.

Now the way was wide open. I went home and started writing that night. I submitted my work to the most widely read, influential psychoanalytical journal in this country, the *Journal of the American Psychoanalytic Association,* about six months later; they accepted it but had several questions on points of fact which I thought were well taken. I asked for a few more months because I wanted to rewrite the whole thing to take care of the questions and add some new material I had found. I resubmitted it in December 1963.

Non-profit journals being what they are, this journal had a large backlog of articles to be published and a rigid rule of publishing them in the chronological order of submission.

So for two years, it seemed that I was sitting back with folded hands—with nothing to do. Actually it was only a few months until I realized how long the wait would be. I started on the research for the next article.

As luck would have it, my piece came out about three months before Masters and Johnson's book appeared. It was nice timing. At the bi-yearly meeting of the psychoanalysts a few months later, Masters and Johnson were asked to present a summary of their findings. They went to the meeting, Dr. Masters later told me, prepared for the worst kind of resistance. "Instead," he said to me, "it seemed that all of them had read your article, and there was no resistance at all. They were eager to explore the implications of the work to greater lengths." I knew then that the first and most important goal had been achieved. I was very pleased.

In the meantime, further evidence of the article's acceptance came pouring in with each mail delivery. Dumbfounded, I answered letters and sent out reprints to psychiatrists, psychologists, and social workers from all parts of the country and from most countries in Western Europe. There was not one letter denouncing the article or arguing with its chief propositions. (I must admit that to this day I have a special stack of letters of congratulation from people you would call the "big names" in psychiatry—men whose work I had studied and admired for so many years—which I keep apart. At times when I get into a miasmic mood, wondering why I keep at this work, I reread these letters and keep working. To be judged and found well by a jury of your more-than-peers is reward, indeed, and balm for all miasmas.)

About a year later, an editor at Random House called me to say that he had read the article and he had shown it to several people at the firm. They wanted me to put the rest of the material into book form. Random House can never know what an enormous relief this offer was for me.

Although I had intended to submit the second section to the *Journal of the American Psychoanalytic Association* I realized by this time that the work was no longer appropriate for that journal. It no longer involved Freudian theories. It contained many animal and anatomical details. And, above all, it contained anthropological and archeological material about the developing sexuality of the Stone Age women. There were at least four major scientific disciplines involved in an interrelated way, so that submitting four separate articles to four different journals did not answer the problem. A book did.

As time went by, it gradually became apparent to my editor and myself that the demand for the material contained in the article that had appeared in the *American Psychoanalytic Journal* was increasing, rather than decreasing. In part this was due to the fact that, in order to continue my research, I had turned down all requests for presentations of the work at professional and non-professional meetings, as well as requests to sit on panels, answer questions for magazines, and the like. (I feared that although Drs. Kinsey and Masters had not been corrupted by fame and fortune, I might be.) Consequently, although the material in the article seemed to seep out slowly, it was gradually gathering momentum as it went. Moreover, the demands of the research had now increased. I cut my practice down as much as I could in order to have more research time. I could no longer afford to send out reprints which were costing more and more. Finally, I was in no hurry to complete the second section for non-personal reasons. The past five or six years had seen the development of new data, especially the results from the work with "the pill" and the rearranging of archeological data because of the new findings on radioactive dating. It seemed that this new research would add considerably more positive evidence to my ideas.

Therefore it was decided that a two-volume publication

was in order, with Volume I being an annotated reprint of the article originally published in the *Journal of the American Psychoanalytical Association,* including this introduction and a glossary. With this publication of Volume I, I would like to offer my sincere apologies to the many people who have written to me for reprints and have not received them.

The wheels of social change grind, if not finely, exceedingly slowly. The task of educating people on these new concepts in biology will slow the movement even more because of the many cultural, religious, and social institutions which have been built for so many centuries on the opposite concepts. Yet cultural changes of this order have occurred before in human history and can occur again—perhaps even in my lifetime.

Mary Jane Sherfey, M.D.

November 9, 1971

CHAPTER 1

Psychoanalytic Theory and the Nature of the Orgasm

A SURVEY OF RECENT DEVELOPMENTS

One of Freud's most useful, accepted, and enduring concepts is his theory of female psychosexual growth with its basic assumption that the female is endowed with two independent erotogenic centers; during development she must transfer the infantile erotogenic zone of the clitoris to the mature erotogenic zone of the vagina.

The clitoral-vaginal transfer theory has been held essentially unchanged by psychoanalysts and psychiatrists in spite of many doubts and objections. The objections are based mainly on four observations: the infrequency of vaginal orgasms in apparently normal women; the lack of sensory nerve endings in the main body of the vagina; the ease with which women can confuse a vaginal orgasm with a clitoral one; and the *seeming* absence of the vaginal orgasm in all subhuman animals. These are certainly cogent reasons but do not necessarily disprove the possibility of the vaginal orgasm.

In fact, we seem to be in a strange dilemma of having a developmental theory that explains so much so well and conforms to so many women's life histories and felt experiences, yet one that has shown surprisingly little therapeutic effectiveness and has had only a questionable basis in biology.

In 1953 Marie Bonaparte (8) made the first mild departure from the "classical" Freudian theory, postulating four gradations of orgastic experiences: the infantile clitoral orgasm alone; the clitoral orgasm with some vaginal sensations; the vaginal orgasm requiring prior clitoral participation; and finally and infrequently, the complete vaginal orgasm with clitoral participation being unnecessary or irritating. The last level of response manifests the peak of mature femininity.

Not until 1954 did a more drastic revision appear in the work of J. Marmor (39). He concluded that the orgasm is always initially clitoral with a "clitoral orgastic center" in the sacral segment of the spinal cord. Emotional and cortical influences playing on this center permit impulses from the clitoris to be transmitted to the vaginal wall, which then contracts to give the vaginal orgasm.*

In 1960, during a panel discussion on the subject of frigidity in women, the predicament was focused by the statements of two well-known psychoanalytic authorities, Ruth Benedek and Helene Deutsch. As reported by B. E. Moore, Benedek stated (51, p. 578):

> . . . female sexuality cannot fit into the male model of sexual maturity upon which psychoanalytic concepts are based. Pregnancy and lactation constitute the completion of psychosexual and reproductive maturity in women,

---

* Marmor's theory has the advantage of being based on evolutionary and adaptational principles and the disadvantage of being based on no acceptable neurological evidence. It requires that a woman must be emotionally prepared to *think* her way into experiencing a vaginal orgasm. Actually, in clinical practice, this does *seem* to be what happens with many patients —an observation which must be explained by any acceptable theory on the nature of the orgasm.

and the drive organization of these phenomena is not "genital" in the same sense as is mating behavior. The expectation that clitoral sensation should be transferred to the vagina is inconsistent with the distribution of the sensory cells responsible for the perception of orgasm.

In spite of this "inconsistency," Benedek still believed that the vaginal orgasm exists, relying on Marmor's theory of the transmission of impulses through the clitoral center in the sacral cord.

On the same panel, Moore recorded Deutsch's opinion (51, p. 571):

Helene Deutsch said that after the publication of her two volumes on female psychology in 1944, consultations, short-term therapy, and other contacts with the subject had given her an opportunity for a macroscopic review of the psychic events and psychopathology which she had previously seen microscopically in analysis. She was shocked by the high incidence of so-called frigidity in women and disappointed in the results of psychoanalytic treatment for it. . . . Considering the complexity of this most primitive function in the human female, Helene Deutsch questioned whether the vagina was really created by nature for the sexual function *we assume and demand for it.* Her own long experience and the lasting impression of Freud's ideas brought her back to the conviction that the female sexual apparatus consists of two parts with a definite division of function. The clitoris is the sexual organ and the vagina primarily the organ of reproduction. The central role of the clitoris is not merely the result of masturbation but *serves a biological destiny.* Into it flow waves of sexual excitement which may be more or less successfully communicated to the vagina. It was Freud's conception, with which she agrees, that although the erotization of the vagina is of course prepared in part biologically, the transition of sexual feeling from the clitoris to the vagina is a task performed largely by the active intervention of the man's sexual organ. The muscular apparatus of the vagina is primarily in the service of reproduction and may or may not become involved in orgastic activity. On the basis of this dualistic conception of the female sexual apparatus, she was ready to reverse the burning question, "Why are women frigid?" to "Why and how are some women endowed with vaginal orgasm?" [Italics added.]

Notwithstanding her question of whether or not the vagina was really created for the function *we assume and demand for it,* Deutsch still accepted the clitoral-vagina transfer theory and ended by giving her opinion that the most "feminine" type of orgasm is one with no orgastic component at all, but one having a passive-receptive sucking-in action, ending in a mild, slow relaxation which brings "complete gratification."

These statements by Deutsch and Benedek strike one as being very revealing of the theoretical predicament and, in a sense, uncommonly courageous, for as Moore succinctly summarized (51, p. 573), their ideas are simply not acceptable to the majority of psychoanalysts who still hold the original Freudian theory valid and view a woman's inability to have a vaginal orgasm always to be evidence of frigidity. Nevertheless, for the first time in psychoanalytic literature, a breach in the fundamental tenets of the clitoral-vaginal transfer theory had been made—albeit a small one.

Since 1960, no further psychoanalytic contributions to the problem of the transfer theory have appeared other than in the work of Heiman.* Heiman utilizes the Masters data to support the transfer theory, the only innovation being the

* See note on p. x.

observation that the orgasm involves only the lower third of the vagina plus strong uterine contractions. Imputing a sucking action to these contractions of vagina and uterus, Heiman makes several correlations between them and sucking on the nipple during infancy.

CULTURAL MANIFESTATIONS OF THE CLITORAL-VAGINAL TRANSFER THEORY

Almost sixty years have passed since Freud's *Three Essays on the Theory of Sexuality* (16). In all these years of brilliant advances in biological knowledge, oddly enough we had no biological proof of whether or not the vaginal orgasm as defined by Freud even existed until strong evidence was gathered over the past nine years by William Masters and Virginia Johnson, and this has not been integrated into psychoanalytic theory. Moreover, there have been no new psychoanalytic contributions to the understanding of female psychosexual development since Freud and the early analysts. The considerable amount of work done has been primarily corroborations and theoretical refinements of the original Freudian concepts. In fact, the whole problem of female sexuality as an area of psychosomatic research has received scant attention. This is most unfortunate, especially since analysts and non-analysts alike must agree with Deutsch and Benedek (51, p. 573 and p. 579) that vaginal frigidity has not decreased with the increased freedom in the upbringing of girls (rather clitoral erotism and fixations seem to have increased) and must agree with Deutsch's conclusion that no form of psychotherapy or analysis has been singularly successful in the treatment of clitoral fixation.

In commenting on marital problems in modern American life, J. L. Schimel (56) expressed the opinion that more and more women (and men) believe that the woman should have an orgasm "just like a man's"—in intensity, duration, frequency, and with mutual timing. I would amplify this psychocultural observation to include a more serious problem: more and more women (and men) accept the equation: vaginal orgasm = normalcy. Hence there is an ever-growing incidence of guilt, fear, and resentments in otherwise healthy women who find themselves unable to achieve the elusive prize.

No doubt every therapist can match Schimel's cases illustrating the inordinate lengths to which couples go in their mutual, sincere, but frenetic efforts to give the woman the "right" kind of orgasm. Another observation fits this picture. Many women seem innocently vague and uncertain when we ask them to describe the nature of their sexual sensations, or they sound like a marriage-manual recitation on the nature of the orgasm. One wonders if this well-known difficulty women have in reporting their sexual sensations does not stem from the fact that they deceive themselves and us about the nature of these feelings—because they are afraid that what they *do* feel is not what they *should* feel.

Finally, there is growing evidence that the predicaments and dilemmas of modern, educated women are rapidly reaching a crisis and may assume proportions revolutionary in their impact on female psychology and the position of women in society. That too many women *are* in a dilemma, are tense, anxious, and uncertain about their identities and social roles, cannot be denied. Since F. Lundberg and M. Farnham's little explosion over the "lost sex" in 1947 (38), the popular literature on "women's predicament" has become a publishing flood. Yet aside from Lundberg and Farnham's initial contribution, Schimel's brief communication, and the few statements by Deutsch and Benedek mentioned earlier, psychiatry seems to have been on the sidelines throughout this spreading social movement. The people laboring to find some answers are those in governmental agencies and college educators on the post-graduate level. I believe they are receiving little support, theoretically or practically, from psychiatry. It is not an exaggeration to say that by reading the psychiatric literature alone one would hardly know the problem exists. Does psychiatry in general and psychoanalysis in particular have nothing to offer to the resolution of the most important problem facing modern women as they react blindly to the forces within their unique society?

While attempting to answer that question, I began reviewing our theories and attitudes on female sexuality several years ago. One strong impression emerged and remained: not just the couples with sexual problems and most of the educated public, but almost all psychiatrists and physicians (excepting gynecologists and endocrinologists) are still committed to the belief in the existence of the vaginal orgasm as distinct from the infantile clitoral orgasm and consider the vaginal orgasm to be a vital sign of normal feminine development.

As we know, it is unfortunately but a step from this belief to the all-inclusive conviction that the vaginal orgasm is *the* sign of a normal and satisfying sexual life, of the possibility for a full and happy marriage, and *ergo* for the most effective and rewarding motherhood. Probably no psychiatrist or analyst would agree to these conclusions—which imply that the fate of womanhood and hence of mankind hangs on the vaginal orgasm—nonetheless it is still true that we have created and fostered this impression. After all, if I am not mistaken, the first printed statement in which a recognized psychoanalytic authority, Benedek, merely "suggested" that the ". . . vaginal orgasm is not necessarily *an indicator* of psychosexual maturity" (51, p. 579; italics added) did not appear until 1961.

The question must be put and answered within the profession: Could the lack of psychiatric interest in the sociopsychological crisis of women today, the absence of deeper levels of understanding of the feminine personality, its functions and dysfunctions, and our serious therapeutic limitations and tragic failures stem, in part, from erroneous assumptions of vaginal and clitoral responsivity which form the basis of the clitoral-vaginal transfer theory? Could many of the sexual neuroses which seem to be almost endemic to women today be, in part, induced by doctors attempting to treat them?

If so, we have before us impressive proof of the extraordinary reach and depth of Freud's thinking, touching the minds of almost everyone. If so, we also have before us the formidable obstacle of a large block of professional and public opinion which exists because people *want* the vaginal orgasm to exist. If so, to dispel these erroneous concepts, we must first dispel them from the minds of psychoanalysts and psychiatrists. To accomplish this requires *indisputable* proof that *the vaginal orgasm as distinct from the clitoral orgasm* does not exist and that whatever does exist instead is compatible with the many observations on female psychosexuality we know to be true. If such proof is forthcoming, the pyschoanalytic theory may not necessarily be refuted but will require amendations.

The question of the existence or nonexistence of the vaginal orgasm is a biological problem and must be answered by biology. This initial study attempts to marshal the biological evidence available at present for psychiatric consideration. We must turn our minds from the psyche to the soma long enough to make the biological data now to be presented a part of our felt knowledge—to accept knowledge without feeling its truth is not to know at all.

Taking Helene Deutsch's phrase as a felicitous one, I suggest the data given here will prove the clitoris to be, not a rudimentary nuisance or tragic stumbling block whose functioning must be transcended or transferred, but a sexual structure of, perhaps, *high biological destiny*. This study has turned out to be an unforeseen and surprising statement on the nature and intensity of the sexual drive in women and an explication of the biological destiny of clitoral erotism in the functioning of the individual and in the evolution of man.

CHAPTER 2

Embryology and the
Nature of Bisexuality

THE CLASSICAL CONCEPT OF BISEXUALITY

One of the biological theories of the nineteenth century most thoroughly integrated into medicine and psychiatry has been the theory of the innate, embryonal bisexuality of all vertebrates. Much of psychoanalytic theory is ultimately based on this biological "truism." However, Freud's application of the theory has come under sharp criticism (6, 21, 29, 53, 54); his concepts have undergone certain ramifications by later analysts not in accord with the facts; and most significantly, psychiatric theory in general has not taken cognizance of the basic changes in the theory necessitated by the recent discoveries in the field of primary sexual differentiation.

First, a brief restatement of the biological premises of Freud's theory of female sexual development will clarify the points at issue. Contrary to the criticism of A. Kardiner et al., I cannot agree that Freud made an "arbitrary leap" (29, p. 212) from the soma of the undifferentiated embryo to the psyche of the infant and adult on the basis of tautologies and wishful thinking. His logic was based on sound, medically accepted embryological theories (some of which have been disproved only in the past five years) coupled with a series of astute, original clinical observations and common-sense conclusions which appeared to admit of no other explanation. Freud's biology can be put very briefly:

1. The undifferentiated embryo had been discovered to be innately bisexual (and not by Freud—some of his critics write as if Freud invented the undifferentiated embryo). After sexual differentiation occurs, male and female structures evolve unequally with one or the other dominating. Hence everyone remains bisexual to some degree.

2. The clitoris is the homologue of the penis but does not become vestigial; it becomes rudimentary and continues to function throughout infancy and childhood with a functioning precisely like that of the phallus, relative to size. Like the phallus, the clitoris is readily available to stimulation during childhood; the vagina is not. Therefore the clitoris is a small phallus which easily lends itself to participation in the total identification processes and body-image formation occurring during development and to all the prelogical thinking of which a little girl's imagination is capable. From here, Freud proceeded to his well-known theories of female infantile sexuality, all of which follow logically given these basic premises. In short, because the girl has a masculine homologue that is the primary source of sexual stimulation during childhood, she will necessarily have more difficulties with her innate bisexuality than the boy who has no comparable functioning feminine homologue.

3. The vagina is a singularly female possession. Until quite recently, it was believed to form from the uterine segment of the oviducts after differentiation has occurred; hence the main body of the vagina would not have even a vestigial counterpart in the male.

4. The vagina must be a second erotogenic zone supplied to females because:

a. Vaginal sensations are practically absent in childhood, while clitoral sensations are patently present. Vaginal sensations normally begin in adulthood with the first coitus, or soon thereafter, and are experienced only during the sexual act.

b. Women with vaginal orgasms unanimously report that the orgastic sensations begin inside the vagina as the result of penile friction against the vaginal walls. Normally, when vaginal erotism takes over, clitoral erotism seems to recede to less and less importance. It apparently disappears entirely in some women.

c. Clitoral activity is entirely different from vaginal erotism and fosters active, narcissistic, and masculinelike behavior. It is capable of providing satisfaction exclusive of any relationship with a man. Vaginal erotism is passive and necessarily receptive, dependent upon the male for its expression. Clitoral activity may exclude motherhood; vaginal receptivity is necessary for it.

d. In by far the majority of women with disturbed relationships with men, clitoral erotism is regularly retained and the capacity for a vaginal orgasm is not achieved. This is almost always true of female homosexuals.

These are the biological premises upon which Freud built his theory of female sexuality. Other than the last point, there are few people today who could convincingly dispute any of them. I believe that psychoanalysis has not made significant changes in the original Freudian concepts because it could not ignore these basic biological premises.

Simple logic then dictated to Freud the conclusion that with maturity the clitoral erotogenic center of childhood must be transferred to the vaginal erotogenic center of adulthood. Thus it was that vaginal erotism became the goal (and symbol) of maturity. (Of course, we understand this to mean that vaginal erotism is only one of the beneficial by-products of maturity. Nevertheless, since sexual adjustment is such an important problem in every single human being at one time or another in his life and so evidently important to marital accord, people in general—and often psychiatrists —tend to blur distinctions between goal, symbol, cause, effect, and by-product.) For Freud, the woman's entire personality is colored and complicated by the dual nature of her sexuality with its fundamental struggle in childhood and early adolescence to relinquish the active, aggressive, masculine sexual pleasure emanating from infantile clitoral activity, which in turn is the result of the innately bisexual nature of the embryo, i.e., clitoral erotism is the remaining functional, masculine component after differentiation of the female has occurred and must undergo still further regression to practically a vestigial state before the fullest maturity can be reached.

The biological aspects of Freud's thinking have been expanded by other analysts in two directions. One stresses the erroneous embryological concept that the penile-clitoral tubercle of the early embryo develops from the urogenital sinus which provides the urethra to the penile shaft; hence "phallic" qualities can be attributed to all the structures in the female derived from both the tubercle and the urogenital sinus (clitoris, labia minora, vestibule, greater vestibular glands and the lower portion of the vagina).* This tendency is exemplified by S. Lorand (37), who termed the lower third of the vagina "anatomically vestibular and pleasure-physiologically phallic."

From here, it is hardly another step to regard all the female external genitalia as more or less miniature structures derived from male anlagen, the primordial structures from which the adult male genitalia grow. (That the reverse

---

* Actually the genital tubercle rises from mesodermal cells migrating from the primitive streak into the space between the ectoderm of the body wall and endoderm of the urogenital sinus long before the sinus has differentiated from the cloaca (64, p. 110).

could be true, i.e., the penis is an exaggerated clitoris, the phallus is "pleasure-physiologically clitoral," the scrotum is derived from the primordial cells of the labia majora, etc., has, until recently, never been given the least consideration.) Bonaparte (8) carried this line of thinking to its logical conclusion, postulating that since the female retains a rudimentary masculine clitoris, relinquished with such difficulty, the basic libido of the external genitalia is innately masculine. All women are burdened with the extremely difficult task of shifting not only from the clitoris to the vagina, but also from an innately masculine sexual drive to an acquired passive and, in many ways, masochistic feminine sexual drive. This whole line of thought essentially states that normal feminine sexuality is derived from an innately masculine sexuality. Thus it is that psychoanalytic theory has led us through a series of perfectly logical steps to a position which is, in essence, anachronistic: a scientific restatement of the Eve-out-of-Adam myth.

(But we must not forget that this theoretical development was amply fostered by many findings from endocrinology, such as the fact that all the external genitalia of the female, except the vagina, are highly responsive to the male sex hormone, androgen—conversely, the male genitalia are highly resistant to female sex hormones.)

Freud's basic premises have been expanded in another direction, as developed by Marmor's theory and the quoted conclusions of Deutsch and Benedek. Clitoral activity has here been admitted partially, as it were, into the process of producing the vaginal orgasm. Since we cannot expect to dispense totally with clitoral erotism, the transfer process now becomes a relay system. Nerve impulses must still be transferred to the vagina by way of the clitoral center in the spinal cord. However, achievement of the vaginal orgasm with a minimum of prior clitoral stimulation remains the ultimate goal—unfortunately achieved by only a few women.

This train of logic relies on the deduction reached by biologists that the vaginal orgasm is a recent evolutionary acquisition. Subhuman animals are thought to experience no orgasm at all or only clitoral ones; most women experience the clitoral climax; and a few women are sufficiently evolved neurologically and integrated psychologically so that their higher cortical impulses can play on the lower sacral center enhancing excitation and effecting the transferral of impulses from clitoris to the vaginal musculature.

Thus the original Freudian transfer theory has now become almost a statement of female psychosexual development as an evolutionary ideal toward which most women must still strive. Only a few superior women have the highly evolved or trained cortex necessary to produce the vaginal orgasm. Therefore vaginal orgastic competency becomes a function of the higher centers and the intellect. Again we are led by clear logic to the very uncomfortable position stating that the majority of women remain biologically inferior, retarded in their psychosexual evolution compared to men, not sufficiently evolved emotionally and intellectually to achieve the vaginal orgasm—albeit all possibilities are open for them to catch up in the near evolutionary future— but they are still more highly evolved than the animals. (Just why all men and all male animals, even those with a bare cortical minimum, should have an orgasm so easily is not clarified; nor is the ease of the male animal's performance correlated with the related concept that the human male has evolved the highest degree of cortical control of sexuality.)

We must not forget that this development was amply fostered, and indeed, was initiated, by data from biology which presumably proved that man *can* exert high cortical dominance over his sexuality, while women have less cortical control than man; that a phylogenetic series* does exist from

---

* *phylogenetic series:* representative examples from developing evolutionary changes of a species or part. (See glossary.)

the lower mammals to man: as more of man's functions migrated from involuntary to voluntary, hormonal influences over sexual activities decreased. Proposed by F. A. Beach (5) in 1948, this attractive hypothesis was quickly and widely accepted, especially in anthropology and psychiatry (14, 32, 35, 52). Beach's hypothesis, so complimentary to man's ego, was not refuted until 1958 by L. R. Aaronson (1). Endocrinologists no longer believe that such a phylogenetic series exists (18, p. 373; 34, p. 150; 66, p. 1207). On the contrary, it has been shown that many animals display variations of "cortical dominance" over hormonal action quite comparable to man's.* In fact, the past ten years have seen a remarkable growth of animal experimentation demonstrating the profound influence of the "learning process," i.e., psychological factors, on gonadal functioning, instinctive behavior, and sexual performance in many animal species (7, 14, 19, 40, 66).

Naturally, extensive criticism has been leveled at these various uses to which psychoanalytic theory has put the concept of embryonic bisexuality. However, the dilemma does not lie in the overimaginative theorizing of psychoanalysts, as many critics imply. The theories offered in place of the psychoanalytic ones are inadequate† or say the same

* For that matter, it can also be shown that man exhibits rigidities of sexual behavior quite comparable to those of animals. It seems that Alfred Kinsey was right (30, p. 446): "exceedingly few males modify their attitudes on matters of sex or change their patterns of overt behavior in any fundamental way after their middle teens. Many individuals do acquire certain details of activity in their later years, and some individuals think that they acquired entirely new attitudes on matters of sex, at some period in their lives. Upper level individuals like to think that they have become more liberal, sexually emancipated, free of former inhibitions, rational instead of traditional in their behavior, ready to experiment with anything. It is notable, however, that such emancipated persons rarely engage in any amount of actual behavior which is foreign to the pattern laid down in their youth."

† For example, J. L. Hampson and J. G. Hampson (21) delivered a massive criticism of Freudian theory because it relies too much on the "in-

thing in different ways. More important, none of them deals with the biological realities: all women *do* have a seemingly rudimentary penis; it *is* the primary source of maximum sexual arousal in childhood; its very presence and functioning *are* the result of genetic, evolutionary adaptations; and clitoral fixation very obviously can, and very often does, interfere with vaginal functioning. The dilemma lies in the erroneous basic premises supplied to psychiatry by biology, a significant part of which has been corrected only in the past few years. None of the alternative theories to the psychoanalytic one has made use of this new biological information.

It is to be hoped that the corrected and startlingly different understanding of the nature of primary sexual differentiation will place the theory of female psychosexual development and the nature of bisexuality on a firmer basis. In the inductor theory of sexual differentiation we have, indeed, an example of that surprising biological information which Freud predicted—and about which he could not have dreamed.

THE INDUCTOR THEORY OF PRIMARY SEXUAL DIFFERENTIATION

The most important contribution from modern comparative embryology to psychiatry is the elucidation of the process of

---

stincts," which the Hampsons seem to think mean constitutional and immutable forces. Impressed with the importance of the first three years of life in establishing the "gender role," and in an effort to get away from the misused term "bisexuality," they proposed the theory that the fetus and neonate are not bisexual, but display a "complete psychosexual neutrality." Since "neutrality" means here what it seems to mean—of neither sex—I cannot see that the theory helps simply because it is not true.

(It is impressive to find that after being roundly castigated for years because they did not pay enough attention to constitutional factors in personality development and disorders, psychoanalysts are now being roundly castigated for having paid too much attention to them!)

primary sexual differentiation and its relationship to the evolution of the bearing of live young. While many psychiatrists may be familiar with this theory, others no doubt are not; and its fundamental facts have not been integrated into psychiatric theory. To begin this integration, the inductor theory* is now presented in sufficient detail to support its conclusions and to advance certain theoretical possibilities related to psychosexual development.†

Strictly speaking, we can no longer refer to the "undifferentiated" or "bisexual" phase of initial embryonic existence. The early embryo is not undifferentiated: "it" is a female. In the beginning, we were all created females; and if this were not so, we would not be here at all.

Genetic sex is established at fertilization; but the influence of the sex genes is not brought to bear until the fifth to sixth week of fetal life (in humans). During those first weeks, all embryos are morphologically females. If the fetal gonads are removed before differentiation occurs the embryo will develop into a normal female, lacking only ovaries, regardless of the genetic sex.‡

If the genetic sex is male, the primordial germ cells arising in the endoderm of the yolk sac and hindgut migrate to the gonadal medulla (future testes) during the fifth week of

---

* The basic research on this theory was done by the French endocrinologist, Jost (28), in 1950, using the rabbit. Its expansion to include all mammals had to await the Barr chromosome test, first used in 1957, which permits the identification of the genetic sex from any of the body cells.

† Except where otherwise indicated, all data on the inductor theory are taken from recent reviews on the subject by four of the outstanding contributors to its development: M. L. Barr, R. H. Burns, J. J. Van Wyk, and E. Witschi (3, 9, 60, 65).

‡ In animal embryos so operated on, a female with male chromosomes but no ovaries will remain physically infantile because the pubertal transformations set off by ovarian functioning cannot occur. These changes can be induced by the administration of the appropriate hormones.

embryonic life. Once there, they stimulate the production of a "testicular inductor substance" which stimulates medullary growth and the elaboration of fetal androgen which suppresses the growth of the Mullerian ducts (oviducts) and the gonadal cortex (ovaries); subsequently fetal androgen induces the rest of the internal and external genital tract into the male growth pattern. Externally this becomes barely evident by the seventh week or a little later. From the seventh to the twelfth week, the full transformation of the male structures is slowly accomplished. After the twelfth week, the masculine nature of the reproductive tract is fully established; sex reversals of these tissues are then no longer possible. (Suppression of growth and function can take place, of course, throughout life.) The time limits during which reversals can occur vary considerably in the different species relative to the life spans. Within each species, the critical period of sexual differentiation is remarkably constant in its time limits and remarkably sensitive to the exact quantity of the heterologous hormone required to effect reversal.

If the genetic sex is female, the germ cells arrive at the gonadal cortex (ovaries) and eventually stimulate the production of the primordial nest of cells and fetal estrogens. However, these estrogens are not necessary for the continued feminization of the reproductive tract. If the gonads are removed before the seventh week so that no estrogen is produced, the embryo will still develop normal female anatomy. No ovarian inductor substance or estrogens are elaborated because none are needed. Female differentiation results from the innate, genetically determined female morphology of all mammalian embryos.

That the circulating maternal estrogens do not cause female differentiation has been demonstrated by ingenious experiments in which embryonic reproductive tracts are entirely removed, kept alive *in vitro* sufficiently long for the critical period to be completed. The growth pattern in all embryos remains female. However, just as androgen is needed for the fullest elaboration of the male pattern, so estrogens are required for the full development of the female pattern. It is not known to what extent the circulating maternal estrogens are involved in this task of secondarily "exploiting" the female pattern. Fetal ovaries could well play an insignificant role, and maternal estrogens an important one, at least for some organs. For example, both male and female human neonates have enlarged breasts which subside to the infantile level by the second postnatal week—in both sexes, the breasts may even secrete a few drops of milk, i.e., "witch's milk" (20, p. 306). It would seem that the maternal estrogens strongly affect male and female embryos to fairly equal degrees.

Therefore only the male embryo is required to undergo a differentiating transformation of the sexual anatomy; and only one hormone, androgen, is necessary for the masculinization of the originally female genital tract.* Female development is autonomous.

RELATIONSHIP TO VIVIPARITY

The only theory explaining the autonomous female anatomy involves the evolution of the bringing forth of live young (9). In the most primitive vertebrates, fishes and amphibia, both androgen and estrogen are utilized for sexual differentiation.† Here the embryo is truly bisexual bipo-

---

* The idea that only one hormone is utilized in the sexual differentiation of rats was proposed as far back as 1934 by B. P. Wiesner (62) on theoretical grounds, but was neither proved nor applied to all mammals until 1950.

† Apparently some species of amphibians are similar to fishes, some to birds, and some to mammals. Actually there are a few species in all the vertebrate orders which have evolved, or are beginning to evolve, the mammalian pattern.

tential, undifferentiated, neutral, etc. But having gonads with a male medulla and female cortex of an initial equipotentiality has its drawbacks. There is a very high incidence of hermaphroditism in these animals. An initial dysbalance between medulla and cortex would insure more certain sexual differentiation.

This was first achieved during the evolution of reptiles and birds by the simple expediency of making all the embryos of reptiles and birds innately *males*. (The complex changes underlying this "expediency" are quite unknown.) No further hormonal activity is needed in genetic males; but all genetic females must elaborate fetal estrogens early in order to be differentiated from the basic male anatomy. If the gonads of birds are removed before differentiation has occurred, all embryos will *remain* males regardless of genetic sex (9, p. 135).

Obviously the pattern of reptiles and birds would not do for those premammalian warm-blooded reptiles where natural selection operated so strongly for increased intramaternal growth time. With estrogen the differentiating hormone, prolonged exposure to the circulating maternal estrogens would feminize all male embryos. Hence an early adaptation to permit normal male development had to be the avoidance of prolonged maternal estrogenic influences. This was accomplished by the simple expediency of changing the autonomous male embryo with estrogenic induction of females into the autonomous female embryo with androgenic induction of males.

In this way prolonged intra-uterine life became possible; instead of bearing eggs we became able to bear live young while not feminizing the male embryo.

Sexual Dimorphism

The inductor theory of sexual differentiation explains many endocrinological and clinical puzzles.* A significant aspect of the theory stems from the fact that not only the primordial gonad but the primordia of all mammalian sexual organs are innately female. Burns (9, p. 145) states:

> . . . in the absence of the gonads, or of any hormonal conditioning, the embryonic sex primordia collectively follow the female pattern of development. In all castrates, regardless of sex, the external genitalia and the derivatives of the urogenital sinus are of the female type, the Mullerian ducts persist and continue in a virtually normal fashion, whereas the Wolffian ducts undergo involution. Thus castrates of either sex toward term have female genital systems which are anatomically complete and almost as well developed as in normal females.

The morphogenesis of the sexual primordia with differentiation is not *imposed* upon the tissues by one hormone or the other; rather, morphogenesis is a function of the genetically determined, innate patterns of somatic organization, with each organ capable of being *exploited* or *inducted* by the hormones within set limits. The hormones serve merely to exaggerate or suppress tendencies of growth inherent in the organization of each primordium (9, p. 139). In effect, this organizational pattern is initially "given" in the female; it must be "acquired" in the male.

* The role of the pituitary in these and other processes is not included in this study. Apparently the pituitary plays no role in the induction of sexual differentiation. It is, of course, decisive once differentiation is established. Both pituitary and other neural factors are omitted solely to keep the material within manageable limits. Therefore, I am dealing only with the reactions of the target organs to the gonadal hormones.

In their somatic organization, the gonads always retain a greater or lesser amount of the opposite-sex tissue which remains functional throughout life. The amount of androgen-producing tissue developed by the ovaries (and adrenals) and the amount of estrogen-producing tissue retained by the testes (and adrenals) are genetically fixed and species-specific. Consequently there is a continuous production of estrogens and androgens by both sexes, although with a preponderance of one or the other. In this way, the degree of sexual dimorphism, i.e. the differentiation of male and female adult forms, is brought to expression. In many lower vertebrates and a number of mammals (especially primates), the genetic code calls for a close to equal amount of functional gonadal medulla and cortex, so that males and females are not very different. In other species, the dysbalance is so great that males and females hardly seem to belong to the same species.

In this connection (i.e., the retained existence of tissue of the opposite sex concurrent with a differentiation of male and female forms), it is important to realize that the mammalian male embryo must elaborate extremely large quantities of androgen throughout fetal life to overcome both its own innate female anatomy and the effects of the circulating maternal estrogens. Consequently after differentiation is completed, male embryos show, and continue to show, a high "resistance" to estrogens injected experimentally, requiring large amounts before feminizing effects appear. Obviously the reverse holds for females where the female anatomy is genetically set, not hormonally determined. Small amounts of androgen, probably only slightly more than enough to overcome the maternal estrogens, will have strong masculinizing effects. All mammalian females tested —embryos, infants, and adults—are appreciatively more reactive to androgen than the males are to estrogens. Thus the often-quoted assertion that because the female's genitalia are so much more responsive to androgens than the male's to estrogens she must be more innately masculine is fallacious. The exact opposite conclusion is true: she is more androgen-responsive because of her innate femaleness which requires little or no estrogens to counteract injected androgens. These relative differences in the requirements for estrogens in the females and androgens in males are maintained proportionately throughout life; hence I suggest we may properly speak of the female's relatively "easy androgen-responsivity" based on the genetically determined nature of the female reproductive tract.

An additional aspect of differentiation should be stressed. Of the entire primordial reproductive tract, the Mullerian and Wolffian ducts (oviducts and vas deferens) are believed to be the only basically dimorphic structures. This belief is based on the time of their separate origins, the latter from the embryonic kidneys and the former probably from peritoneal evaginations. Normally one or the other becomes vestigial or disappears entirely. The gonads, the rest of the genital tract, and all secondary sexual characteristics begin as unimorphic, female structures, which must undergo further differentiation in males. The suppression of the female duct system in males must also be accomplished by fetal androgens; but the suppression of the male duct system in females is not accomplished by fetal—or maternal—estrogens. This too is an innately determined process. The male ducts are suppressed even when they are removed from the body and kept alive *in vitro,* thereby removed from all hormonal influence. Whether taken from a genetic female or male embryo, these two pairs of entirely isolated duct systems will develop into the female oviducts while the male duct system completely degenerates.

Precisely, it is only with these originally dimorphic structures, the duct systems, that the opposite-sex system will have no use at all in adult life. Organs growing from the originally unimorphic, female primordial cells, however, will have functional value in both sexes; all are retained and grow into whatever modified form is compatible with the function to be served.

Figure 1 shows a seven-week human genital tract taken from an embryo which is just entering the differentiation stage (58). This one happens to be a female, but its gender could be determined up to this point only by the Barr chromosome test. It is clear that the large genital tubercle (glans and corpora cavernosi), the labioscrotal folds, the urethral-labial folds, and vestibule are all well defined and clearly female in form and general configuration.

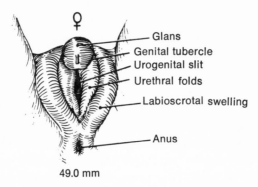

Glans
Genital tubercle
Urogenital slit
Urethral folds

Labioscrotal swelling

Anus

49.0 mm

Figure 1. Female external genitalia, 49 mm. embryo, c. 7 weeks. Reproduced from illustration by Spaulding (58), as adapted by J. J. Van Wyk. In *Textbook of Endocrinology*, 3rd ed., by R. W. Williams, Philadelphia: W. B. Saunders Company, 1961. Reproduced by courtesy of Carnegie Institution of Washington.

Theoretical Perspectives

The concept of innate embryonic bisexuality must be amended. Female development pursues a straight course with the reproductive organs not subjected to any hormonal differentiating transformation. Fetal and maternal estrogens merely enhance, and this later, slowly, and to a relative moderate degree, the already unfolding female morphology. On the other hand, strong activity from fetal androgen is necessary to change the female morphology into the masculine pattern; hence male development "can be considered as a deviation from the basic female pattern" (20, p. 306). The male may be said to go through a "bisexual" or "hermaphroditic" hormonal stage, I suppose, as the increasing production of androgen gradually overcomes the innate female anatomy and the maternal estrogens, veering the female structures into the male growth direction. But any true bisexual stage would be impossible to pinpoint—a fleeting moment in time during which female and male hormonal influences are equal; but this would occur at different moments for different organs and for different species. In humans, by the end of the second fetal month at the latest, the masculine deviation is externally apparent; by the end of the third month, it is complete.

Therefore the primacy of the embryonic female morphology forces us to reverse long-held concepts on the nature of sexual differentiation. Embryologically speaking, it *is* correct to say that the penis is an exaggerated clitoris, the scrotum is derived from the labia majora, the original libido is feminine, etc. The reverse is true only for the birds and reptiles. For all mammals, modern embryology calls for an Adam-out-of-Eve myth!

It is unfortunately true, I believe, that had the traditional view been substantiated by embryology—and all embryos were innately males from which the females derived—a large number of people would have loudly leaped to the conclusion that such was unassailable proof of the innately masculine nature of the sexual drive, clear evidence for the scientific affirmation of the Eve-out-of-Adam myth, and "objective" confirmation of masculine superiority argued from the logic of original creation. I mention this (I trust unnecessarily) in order to obviate such misguided claims now, especially from outside the profession, of innate female superiority based on a biological original-creation myth, which would be totally unscientific and simply foolish.

The original mammalian femaleness came about as a biological necessity and carries all the biological appropriateness so regularly seen in adaptive changes. Evolution is only "concerned" that a necessary and sufficient degree of sexual differentiation and distinction exists in each species to insure species survival. Which sex differentiates from which is immaterial.

With this understanding of evolutionary and embryological development, one conclusion must force itself upon psychiatric theory: *to reduce clitoral erotism to the level of psychopathology because the clitoris is an innately masculine organ or the original libido is masculine in nature must now be considered a travesty of the facts.*

Moreover, of all the external genitalia of the female, only the clitoral shaft has become extremely small in size. The crura and the bulbs of the vestibule with their respective muscles continue to grow in proportion to body size in females as do their homologues in males. An explication of the reduction of clitoral shaft size during evolution will be detailed at a later time. Suffice it to say now, reduction in shaft size with the retention of a large crural and bulbar apparatus was a positive adaptation, probably occurring relatively late in primate evolution, which enhanced female sexuality rather than lessened it and was an important link in the chain of adaptational events leading to human sexuality.

Until biology returns new answers to us, we must accept as a fundamental fact that the mammalian sexual organs begin existence as anatomically and physiologically female structures with all the potentialities for development in the female growth pattern. If the genetic code then so dictates, these female structures are transformed into male sexual organs by the action of fetal androgens.

The innate femaleness of mammalian embryos was firmly established between 1957–58 (with, of course, over fifteen years of prior research); but the biologists recorded the fact with little comment. Although some of us might question the motivation behind their lack of interest in this startling discovery which overturns centuries of mythology and years of scientific theory, it could be expected, since the biologists had long considered the "bisexuality" of the "undifferentiated" phase to be of no prime importance.* To them, adult sexuality was an expression of all the genderizing forces of which the balance of hormones *after* differentiation was only one key factor (36).

INNATE FEMALENESS AND ADULT SEXUAL STRUCTURES AND BEHAVIOR

We are faced, then, with the somewhat paradoxical situation in which the innate femaleness of mammalian embryos is the precondition for the female's ready androgen responsivity. To my knowledge, no one has asked if there is any relationship between adult sexual functioning and this precondition and responsivity. An adequate exploration of the possible relationships is not appropriate to the present study;

* This discovery is certain to create severe resistance. Thus far the resistance has appeared in three ways (and by the majority of scientists writing about sexual differentiation): (a) ignoring the first six weeks altogether or retaining the old terms "undifferentiated" or "neutral" for the period. Surely a somewhat comical level obtains when one finds such statements as, "The neutral sex is female"; (b) dismissing the subject with terse jargon, i.e., "the male is homogametic and the female is heterogametic"; and (c) stressing that androgen is the active, differentiating hormone with no hint of what happens to the genetic male in the absence of androgen or why.

however, it is essential to stress certain aspects of primate sexuality which, I believe, stem from this fundamental androgen reactivity and, in any event, must be involved in the evolution of the sexuality of the human female.

In every species, selection exploits the available anatomical and physiological characters to enhance reproductive success. The great diversity of structuring which the sexual hormones have achieved in creating the secondary sexual characteristics is an obvious example. One would expect the easy androgen reactivity of mammalian females to be manifested throughout the order.

For years biologists have considered the so-called primitive nature of the external genitalia of many primate females (i.e., the high incidence of retention of seemingly masculinelike structures) to be due to the retarded evolution of the primates, which made the appearance of man from a nonspecialized and fairly primitive stock possible. However, if we think of the clitoral complex with its large embryonic shaft and glans as female throughout mammalian ontogeny* and phylogeny† and if we realize that the adaptive exploitation of the female's androgen responsivity would lead to "masculinelike" characters used solely in the interest of procreative success, the "masculinelike" primitive conception of the female's genitalia loses all significance. It is interesting to note that while the so-called masculinelike genitals occur in every mammalian order, the three orders in which they are the most evident are those with the highest degree of reproductive success, both in terms of evolutionary longevity and in the number of living species and members. These are the Insectivora, containing some of the oldest known species, and the Rodentia and the Primates, which contain two of the most recently evolved examples of spectacular reproductive success: mice and

* *Ontogeny:* the embryonic developmental growth of the individual.
† *Phylogeny:* the evolutionary development of a species.

men. It does not seem biologically plausible that such marked reproductive success could be achieved by so many species in which the all-important link in the chain, the female's reproductive tract, remained relatively primitive and evolutionarily stagnant.

The unique advantages for reproductive success from an enhanced androgen reactivity is evident in many mammalian species but is particularly so in certain primates. In these animals, the androgen production by ovaries, adrenals, and placenta is very high. *In many primate species, the females would be diagnosed hermaphrodites if they were humans.* In no other mammalian group do we find the coincidence of the so-called masculinelike genitals, the very prolonged intra-uterine life, single offspring, prolonged lactation and infancy, and the strong socialization of the males into a closely knit and highly organized social structure. It must be stressed that the "masculinization" of the genitalia of these primate females has no adverse effect on the quality of their maternal care. On the contrary, they make excellent mothers; and except when reared in enforced social isolation and sensory deprivation, their adult sexuality is universally and completely of the "vaginal-receptive" type.

This illustrates the truth of the statement that there is no clear-cut dichotomy between the physiological or behavioral effects of estrogens and androgens (66, p. 1193). Rather, the innately female morphology of the primate female has been molded by selection pressures toward increased androgen sensitivity while remaining totally in the service of female sexuality and procreation. We may have difficulty conceiving it, but natural selection has no difficulty using sexually heterotypic structures for homotypic purposes. For example, progesterone is the "pregnancy hormone," essential for menstruation and the prolonged pregnancy. It is as uniquely a "female" hormone as one can be. Yet progesterone possesses strong androgenic properties. It may be used to masculinize female embryos. In 1960, Jones

(27, 63) demonstrated that progesterone given to human mothers early in pregnancy to prevent threatened miscarriages by decreasing uterine motility was most effective for that purpose but also severely masculinized a female fetus. Moreover, progesterone and 17–hydroprogesterone* are the precursors of both estrogens and testosterone (55) and are essential links in the biosynthesis of all the steroid hormones.

The sexuality of primate females shows four characteristics closely related to their androgen responsivity. The first is the remarkable evolution of the clitoral system *in conjunction with* the evolution of the vagina. Secondly, the evolution of the single pair of pectoral mammae occurred concomitantly with the evolution of the diverse skin secondary sexual characteristics and the development of the intense skin erotism. (The biologists do not seem to appreciate that the mutual grooming so important in the evolution of primate social life is based on their skin erotism.) Thirdly, the evolution of the massive estrus perineal edema, the "sexual skin," made its appearance. Finally, and probably as a result of the first three, there arose the long monthly periods of estrus responsivity. Together, or in various combinations, these four features engendered in certain species *an extraordinarily intense, aggressive sexual behavior and an inordinate orgasmic capacity* not equaled by any other mammalian female. In the next volume, I will show the development of the clitoral system, skin erotism, the sexual skin, and the estrus reactions as the primary preadaptations essential for the evolution of the full menstrual cycle and, in humans, for the escape from ovulation heat to our continuous sexual receptivity and responsivity.

The clitoral system, skin erotism, and the sexual skin create the extremely high levels of sexual tension which impel these females to insist on repeated matings during estrus. Thus the aggressive female mating pattern with its high level

* 17–*hydroprogesterone:* a male hormone similar to progesterone.

of sexual drive becomes an important factor in primate reproductive success. The hormonal combinations producing the anatomical features which create the strongest, most prolonged sexual drive and highest capacity for sexual pleasure are the same hormonal combinations which produce the greatest fertility, the fewest abortions, the most viable offspring, and the healthiest animals. These are the females most dominant in the female social hierarchy, closest to the dominant male(s), and whose healthy offspring are dominant in the juvenile social hierarchy and most likely to become the dominant males and females when adults.

The biologists have tended lately to discount sexuality as a strong evolutionary force, but viewed in the light of the evolution of the innately female genitals and the biological inseparability of sexuality and procreation, the importance of the sexual drive can hardly be denied.

The succeeding portions of this examination are devoted essentially to the conclusion that a potentially similar inordinately high level of sexual drive and orgasmic capacity existing in the primate females continues to exist in women. In fact, the data suggest that the sexual responses of women and these primates are so nearly identical that the significant differences must have evolved only recently. Finally, I will bring in evidence to corroborate the thesis that the suppression by cultural forces of women's inordinately high sexual drive and orgasmic capacity must have been an important prerequisite for the evolution of modern human societies and has continued, of necessity, to be a major preoccupation of practically every civilization.*

---

* This key concept is far from new—it is inherent in the more archaic portions of most mythologies, e.g., Eve and her snake tempting Adam with apples. As a working anthropological thesis, however, it was completely rejected by modern anthropologists (see note on p. 138) because of the lack of evidence except in the symbolisms of the ancient myths.

The implications of this new biological information for psychoanalytic theory become clear. In a very important sense, Freud was right. He had perceived a basic truth but could not develop it accurately with the biological knowledge at his disposal. Females *do* possess a fundamental "masculinelike" sexual drive based on a highly effective clitoral erotism. However, this drive is powered by both androgens and estrogens and is a universal characteristic of all women. It seems that primate females have a genetically determined androgen reactivity which is not paralleled by an equally strong estrogen reactivity in the males. Natural selection has exploited the androgen reactivity of the females producing androgen-sensitive structures which are completely in the service of female sexuality and the procreative process.

In order to substantiate these concepts on the evolution and nature of the human female's sexual drive, it is necessary to know the precise anatomy and physiology of women's sexual system with all the detail and accuracy which we so diligently demand for every other system of the body. Precision in this area of biological research has been conspicuous in its absence. Fortunately, the Masters and Johnson research program has provided us, I believe, with the most accurate and complete information on the sexual responses of women thus far produced.

The observations of these investigators on the actual anatomical changes and the physiodynamics of the sexual cycle in women have far-reaching implications demanding psychiatric attention. A full appreciation of this work is necessary, both for the acceptance of its validity and for the understanding of the evolutionary, psychological, and social conclusions it corroborates. It is predicted that all future developments in the psychoanalytic theory of female psychosexuality will be biologically grounded in the inductor theory of primary sexual differentiation and in the observations of Masters and Johnson on the sexual cycle in women.

CHAPTER 3

Clitoral Erotism and the Sexual Response Cycle in Human Females

As quoted earlier, Deutsch suggested that the clitoris may be a primary organ of sexuality in women. Not that she was the first to propose that the clitoris may play an important, if not the only, role in the orgastic response. For example, C. S. Ford and F. Beach (15) tentatively put forth what amounts to the same idea in their classic cross-cultural, cross-species study, *Patterns of Sexual Behavior,* published in 1951; in spite of certain questionable theories, such as the widely held belief that female mammals do not experience orgasms, this work deserves a signal position among the scientific contributions casting doubt on the clitoral-vaginal transfer theory.

The Kinsey study, *Sexual Behavior of the Human Female* (31), was probably the outstanding contribution in the 1950s to the theory that clitoral erotism is the only erotism in women. Backed by their considerable statistical data, the Kinsey authors state bluntly that their findings confirm the proposition that the vaginal orgasm is a biological impossibility. We cannot lightly dismiss the fact (although we have been doing so) that endocrinologists have maintained since the early 1940s that the clitoris is

normally the primary source of sexual arousal, and androgen the primary sexual hormone in women although not the
only one (50, p. 1390). The same is held by the gynecologists, I believe, although they tended to avoid the issue until
the Masters and Johnson research began appearing in 1959.
The remainder of this book consists of a presentation of the
Masters and Johnson work, thus far published, and a beginning attempt to integrate their observations into a unified
cultural, historical, and psychobiological approach to the
psychosexuality of women.

THE MASTERS AND JOHNSON
RESEARCH PROGRAM

A brief résumé of this unusual research project is in order.
William Masters began ten years ago to collect data on the
observable reactions of women during sexual arousal and
developed a method, using color motion-picture photogra-
phy, of visualizing the vagina during autostimulation and
coitus. Since his first publication on the subject, he has col-
laborated with Virginia E. Johnson, publishing four more
papers on basic research in *The Western Journal of Surgery,
Obstetrics, and Gynecology*. The initial article in that journal was introduced by the editor commending these investigators on the high technical and ethical quality of their research procedures.

After demonstrating the nature of the sexual responses of
women, the authors have made original contributions to
(a) the sexual response cycle in men; (b) the nature of the
functioning of the artificial vagina in two patients with congenital atresia of that organ; (c) the changes in the acidity
level of the vaginal transudate during the sexual cycle and
its relation to fertility; (d) the production of a lethal ovulatory sperm factor in certain cases of infertility; and (e) the
mechanism of the deposition of semen and the physical fac-

tors in both males and females conducive to conception. The present résumé is concerned only with the work on the sexual response cycles with brief references where pertinent to the other findings.

There is a flaw in this research which is more apparent than real. Most of the observations have been carried out on volunteer couples (about 75 per cent are married couples and 25 per cent are single women, most of whom are divorced, separated, or widowed). Interjecting a personal sentiment, I would like to remark that these must be people who not only have complete confidence in Dr. Masters but also are knowledgeable and idealistic enough—with the courage of their convictions—to believe that the results of this research could have a lasting beneficent influence on mankind. In order to protect absolutely their identities (publicity could be quite catastrophic), Dr. Masters has steadfastly refused to release their case histories or any data that might be remotely revealing. Without such safeguards, he could not have carried out this research as he has for ten years. This precautionary measure does mean that we have no way of judging whether or not the sexual cycles observed occur in women with normal psychosexual functioning. While the question could have been legitimate earlier in the program, by now it is rather academic. As we shall see, the same response pattern occurs in all women regardless of character structure and psychopathology—or lack of it.

Another obtruding but predictable variable is the fact that many volunteers must go through an orientation period before they can experience arousal in the presence of the photographic and medical paraphernalia and personnel of a complicated research program. The time required seems surprisingly short (to me): it requires an average of three to six sessions of half an hour each for a volunteer to desensitize to the lack of privacy and the many distractions. Of interest is the finding (41) that women desensitize with

appreciably greater ease than men: 85 per cent of performance difficulties from this cause occurred in the men.

Criticism that the desensitization process and the abnormal environment may create abnormal sexual responses is
forcibly contradicted by three facts: (a) once desensitization has occurred, all women show the same response pattern under all conditions; (b) all subjects unanimously report that their subjective experience is precisely the same as
it was before entering the program and has remained the
same at all times since—or has improved (it is to Masters
and Johnson's great credit that in the ten years of this research not one volunteer has suffered detectable psychic or
psychosexual impairment from the procedures); (c) the
extraordinarily large number of cycles observed now makes
it most unlikely that the reported responses are unusual.

The photographic techniques are available to anyone and
the color films constitute a permanent and convincing rec-
ord from which the Masters and Johnson observations can
be, and have been, amply confirmed by others. There is no
longer doubt that these are the normal sexual responses
of all women which unfold whenever they are sexually
aroused, and which appear with the same regularity of se-
quential events that has long been known to occur in the
sexual cycles of men.

ANATOMY

Before presenting these data, a brief description of the anatomy involved may be helpful to provide a quick reference
for the anatomical details discussed and to serve as a reference for the later section on the evolution of these structures
in the primates.

Judging from the biological, medical, and psychiatric literature (and patients' statements), there is still a widespread tendency to forget that the clitoris is not just the

small protuberance at the anterior end of the vulva.* The
deeper-lying components of the clitoral system are almost
never taken into consideration, let alone the deposition and
size of the veins and muscles surrounding the lower third of
the vagina.†

---

* *Vulva:* the external sexual organs of the female.

† I should further document this rather sweeping generalization. I mentioned earlier that most physicians are committed to a belief in the normalcy of the vaginal orgasm versus the abnormal clitoral orgasm. This
also applies to the biologists. During the past four years, I have made
a fairly extensive review of the sexual anatomy of mammals, especially
the primates. In not one of the works of the comparative anatomists
(including the major German reviews) are the deeper-lying clitoral
structures described—indeed they are not even mentioned! (The
exceptions are the veterinary studies, but even these descriptions are
scant; and since domestic animals are highly bred for reproduction, they
cannot be used to study natural evolution.) Because the comparative
anatomists and biologists do such a thorough job on every other body
system, including the male sexual anatomy, this total omission of the
cryptic clitoral structures is of interest.

I wrote to W. C. Osman Hill, who has authored the first five volumes
of a monumental ten-volume compendium of the anatomy of the primates
(24), without which this present study could not have been done, about
this omission. He kindly replied by giving me some important related
data and references. However, he could offer no explanation for the
omission but stated he would rectify it where possible in his forthcoming
volumes (25). My review of the literature on all mammals convinces me
that the cryptic clitoral anatomy has simply not been looked at. (I am
sure there must be exceptions in the huge biological literature scattered
through many journals in many languages—I am also sure the exceptions
must be infrequent.) The physiologists have been equally unseeing. To
my knowledge, there exists not one endocrinological study on animals
showing the differential responses of the vestibular bulbs to the estrogens,
progestins, or androgens; nor does there exist even a single study on the
relative functioning sizes of these bulbs in different women or animals.

Therefore, I suggest that the biologists are similar to almost everyone
else: we all want the vaginal orgasm to exist and the clitoral orgasm not
to exist. The biologists have banished the offending member by ignoring
its most important anatomy; the psychiatrists have condemned it to ex-
tinction by labeling its adult functioning rudimentary, infantile, and neurotic. Should these deductions turn out to be, in essence, true, it is a telling
comment on the objectivity of psychiatrists—even though we would be in
good company, now and throughout all recorded history, more could
justifiably be expected of us.

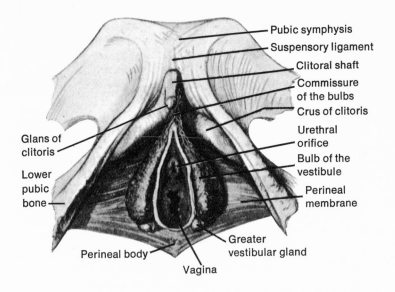

Figure 2. Dissection of female perineum, showing the clitoris, the bulbs of the vestibule, and the greater vestibular glands. From *Cunningham's Textbook of Anatomy,* edited by G. J. Romanes and published by Oxford University Press as an Oxford Medical Publication.

Figures 2, 3, 4, and 6 illustrate the female genital tract; Figure 5 shows the penis, included to indicate differences in sizes and positions of these structures relative to the female homologues. The vestibular bulbs and the commissure completely ring the vaginal orifice except posteriorly (Fig. 2). The entire clitoris lies beneath the urogenital diaphragm and has no neural, muscular, or vascular connections with the vagina except the dense bulbar venous plexus which merges into the vaginal venous plexus (Fig. 6). The plexi are most densely applied along the lateral walls of the vagina, not anteriorly or posteriorly. Note that the muscles of the diaphragm and the levator ani converge on the lateral walls of the lower third of the vagina (Fig. 3), and all unite behind the vaginal orifice to form the perineal body (Fig. 4). The three perineal compartments deserve comment. They allow vaginal expansion; they become obliterated during labor. The lower superficial perineal compartment or fossa contains the bulbs and the crura with their contracting muscles; Figure 3 gives a good idea of the extensive room provided for their expansion. From Figure 4, it is clear that the muscles of the bulbs and crura with the anterior folds of the labia minora (clitoral prepuce) and the rectus abdominus via the suspensory ligament all gain attachment to the clitoral shaft.

Since the cryptic clitoral structures will double or triple in size during sexual arousal (judging from the space provided them), it is apparent why so much functional importance can be attributed to them. On the other hand, the tiny clitoral shaft with its tinier glans comprises only the distal one fourth to three fourths inch of the total clitoris and less than one tenth its volume; this discrepancy is even greater during arousal when the cryptic structures may increase threefold in size, while the shaft and glans hardly do so at all.

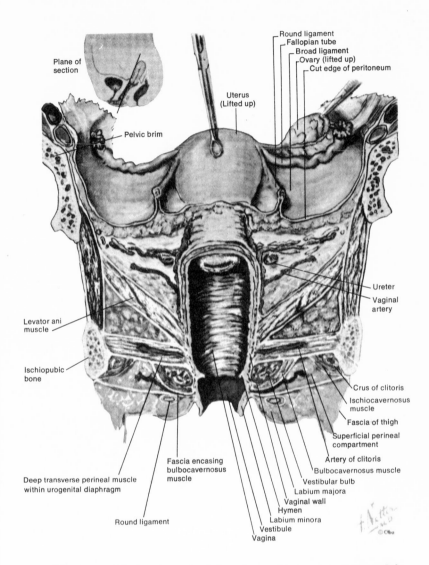

Figure 3. Ligamentous, fascial, and muscle support of the pelvic viscera. Copyright 1954, © 1965, CIBA Pharmaceutical Company, Division of CIBA-GEIGY Corporation. Reproduced, with permission, from THE CIBA COLLECTION OF MEDICAL ILLUSTRATIONS by Frank H. Netter, M.D. All rights reserved.

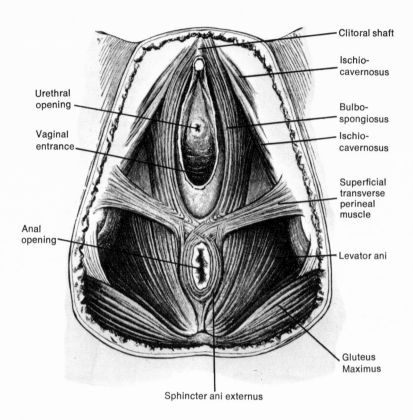

Figure 4. The muscles of the female perineum. (After Peter Thompson.) From *Cunningham's Textbook of Anatomy*, edited by G. J. Romanes and published by Oxford University Press as an Oxford Medical Publication.

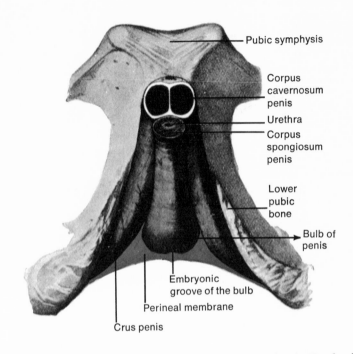

Figure 5. **The root of the penis.** From *Cunningham's Textbook of Anatomy*, edited by G. J. Romanes and published by Oxford University Press as an Oxford Medical Publication.

Evolutionary Perspectives

There are two anatomical observations which, I submit, are important and indicate the many ramifications of these details. First, the penile bulb and its corpora spongiosum in males and the corresponding homologues, the vestibular bulbs and anterior commissure in females, are late evolutionary acquisitions. They first evolved in females as the bilateral bulbs around the vaginal orifice. Secondly, in human males, the length of the penile shaft is remarkably constant, varying less with body size than does any other body part. Conversely, the penile bulb varies considerably in size relative to body size and from one man to another (10, p. 763). Therefore, the size of the distended bulb must play a more important role in producing the intensity of the orgasm than does the length of the erect shaft. (See also p. 77.) The same considerations would apply to the female's vestibular bulbs and clitoral shaft in producing the orgasm.

I propose that in the evolution of these structures, substantial significance must attend the fact that the cryptic clitoral structures have achieved such a large size, only slightly less than the homologous structures in males, relative to body size; whereas the "pendulous" shaft is a disproportionately tiny distal tip. Indeed, the clitoral shaft (corpora cavernosi) looks malformed compared to the size of its crura and the circumvaginal structures (Fig. 2). We know that the shaft is neither rudimentary nor in the least nonfunctional. It engorges during arousal (see p. 83), and the glans is the most sensitive erotogenic zone of the body with its mucous membrane so densely packed with specialized nerve endings it is difficult to see how there could be room for blood vessels. The entire sexual cycle can be set in motion and maintained to orgasm by the lightest stimulation of the glans alone.

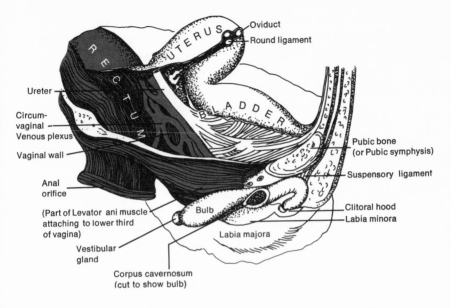

Figure 6. Model of a dissection of the female pelvic organs. Note the size of the vaginal plexus.

No attempt has been made to elucidate the evolutionary significance of this discrepancy in size between the clitoral shaft and the rest of the clitoral complex. In a forthcoming volume, this attempt will be made as well as an effort to show the relationship of the reduction in shaft size to the evolution of the bulbs and the vagina. I will propose that a relationship exists between the reduction in clitoral size, the evolution of the vagina, the menstrual cycle, and the escape from estrus cyclicity along with the evolving modes of human sexual behavior. Considering the importance of the human sexual behavioral patterns and their relevance to our love relationships and social life, these structural details could have far-reaching import for our understanding of man's psychosexuality.

THE SEXUAL RESPONSE CYCLE OF THE HUMAN FEMALE

The average physical responses of the normal sexual cycle of women as observed by Masters and Johnson are summarized in Chart I. The following discussion elaborates on the chart, presents additional data, and gives my interpretations of the data. Masters and Johnson present their findings objectively with few interpretations and no theories. Hence, unless otherwise noted, all interpretations, deductions, and speculations derived from these findings are entirely mine.

SUBJECTS

Masters (41) informs me that, to date, the research team has observed over 4,000 sexual cycles in a total of 321 women (ages: 20–70; parity: 0–5*). The observations were made with subjects in three coital positions: female-supine, female-superior, and knee-chest. Cycles were studied

* *Parity 0–5:* women having borne from zero to five children. (See glossary.)

in which arousal and orgasms were attained by natural coition; autostimulation; use of the artificial phallus; and, in three subjects, by breast stimulation alone. No subject was capable of reaching a climax by fantasies or by reading pornographic literature alone.

1. Similarity of Cycles

Of course, there are wide variations from the charted pattern among different women and in the same woman at different times. However, the variations are those of timing (duration of each phase), intensity of all reactions, differences due to whether or not the woman has borne children and the extent of obstetrical damage, and differences related to the time during the menstrual cycle when arousal occurs. The basic anatomical and physiological responses are always the same, with the responses appearing in their charted sequence uniformly in all women under all conditions of arousal. The authors state (46, p. 254): "From an anatomic point of view, there is absolutely no difference in the response of the pelvic viscera to effective sexual stimulation, regardless of whether stimulation occurs as the result of clitoral area manipulation, natural or artificial coition, or, for that matter from breast stimulation alone. . . . The female's physiologic responses to effective sexual stimulation . . . develop with consistency regardless of the source of the psychic or physical sexual stimulation."

2. Source of Pelvic Sexual Tension

Effective stimulation from any erotogenic source produces an immediate and intense vasocongestion (blood accumulation) of the entire pelvic area, primarily involving the pelvic venous plexi (capillary vasodilatation also occurs in the peripheral circulation, especially in the skin and the breasts). Venous dilation and congestion are quickly followed by the passage of fluid from the venous networks into

CHART I

The Sexual Response Cycle of the Human Female

Summary of Data from Masters, and Masters and Johnson (45–51).

	PHASE I. EXCITEMENT Duration: Several minutes to hours.	**PHASE II. PLATEAU** Duration: 30 seconds to 3 minutes.
SKIN	No Change. (Sexual flush may begin towards end of Phase I.)	Sexual Flush: (Inconstant; most obvious in the fair-skinned.) Papillary rash. First on epigastrium, spreads to breasts, neck & face; may extend over shoulders, down inner surface of arms; may spread onto abdomen, thighs, buttocks & back. Looks like the measles rash.
BREASTS	Changes in order of appearance: 1. Nipple Erection: (Inconstant.) Tumescence may occur in one nipple before the other. 2. Venous Congestion: Increased definition of venous pattern, esp. in large breasts or if marked increase in breast size. 3. Enlargement of Areolae.	1. Sexual Flush: pink mottling on skin coalesces to produce a papillary rash. 2. Breast size increases up to ¼ of normal, esp. in breasts that have not been nursed. 3. Areolae spread laterally; protrude so as to impinge on nipple erection which seems to disappear.
CLITORIS	*GLANS.* No visible change in ½ of subjects; however on colposcopic examination, tumescence always effects a close apposition of glans to its loosely-applied superficial integument. In other ½ of subjects, tumescence up to 2-fold increase in glans diameter appears late in Phase I. (Onset and size of increase varies, related to extent of direct stimulation of mons area. Enlargement of clitoris always parallels that of labia minora.) *Shaft.* Always increases in diameter; extent varies. Elongation (inconstant) in only 10% of subjects.	*Retraction of Clitoris:* retracts from normal pudendal overhang position; withdraws deep into the prepuce carrying frenulum & labia up with it. Stands high on anterior border of symphysis. Just before climax, it is difficult to visualize. Onset earlier with direct mons area stimulation. Reversible: recurs repetitively if Phase II is prolonged with tension falling back to Phase I. Occurs universally. Penile distension of vaginal orifice with thrusting motion stimulates clitoris by pulling on minor labia folds, creating significantly higher levels of sexual tension.
LABIA MAJORA	*Nullipara:* Labia thin down & flatten out against the perineum with slight elevation upwards & out, away from vaginal orifice. *Multipara:* Rapidly increasing vasocongestion & engorgement, esp. if varicosities present. May become 2–3 times normal size by end of Phase I.	*Nullipara:* Labia majora disappear for all clinical purposes. *Multipara:* Labia become so engorged that "they hang like folds of a heavy curtain." (In nullipara, labia may re-swell if Phase II is unduly prolonged.)
LABIA MINORA	*Color Change.* In nullipara, turn bright pink, darkening as Phase II is approached. In multipara, same except color is a bright red. *Size.* In all subjects, congestion causes 2–3 times increase over normal size. (Inner surfaces form continuous channel with the vagina. As Phase II approaches, distended labia add up to 1 inch (ave.=½") of firm sidewall to vaginal length. Widened labia form funnel directing penis into vaginal orifice.	*Color Change.* In nullipara, at maximum swelling, labia suddenly turn a brilliant red. In multipara, same except color is a burgundy red or darker if varicosities marked. (Color Change signifies onset of Phase II; orgasm invariably follows within 3 minutes if stimulation is continued.) *Size.* Enlarge to twice normal size or more. (With intromission, thrusting movements stimulate labia & underlying bulbar complex. Form a sensate focus equal to that of clitoris.)

PHASE III. ORGASM Duration: 3–15 seconds.	PHASE IV. RESOLUTION Duration: with orgasm, 10–25 minutes; with no orgasm, several hours.
No Change. (When present, flush reaches peak with onset of orgasm; degree parallels intensity of orgasm.)	Fine, filmy perspiration, esp. on areas covered by flush. Not related to extent of physical exertion. Flush disappears in reverse order of its appearance.
No Change. (Venous tree pattern stands out in bold relief. Breasts may become tremulous as body goes through the orgasmic experience.)	Return to normal in following order: 1. Loss of Sexual Flush. 2. Detumescence of Areolae leaving nipples erect. 3. Size decreases over 5–10 min. 4. Loss of Venous Tree Patterning. 5. Loss of Nipple Erection.
No Change. (Shaft and glans remain totally retracted and not visible. Thrusting movements continue to produce total clitoral stimulation throughout orgasm. Orgasm stops abruptly if stimulation is stopped.)	Shaft returns to normal overhang position in 5–10 seconds. Glans diameter, if increased, returns to normal in 5–30 minutes as does detumescence of shaft. Extreme sensitivity of glans remains for several minutes: painful to touch. (If no orgasm, clitoris remains engorged for several hours.)
No Change.	*Nullipara:* Labia majora *increase* to normal size in 1–2 minutes or less. *Multipara: Decrease* to normal size in 10–15 minutes with orgasm; requires several hours or more without orgasm.
Proximal portion contracts with contractions of the lower third of the vagina.	Returns to pink color of Phase I in 90–120 secs., giving a blotchy color. Total resolution of color change and of size increase in about 5 minutes. (Decoloration of labia, loss of clitoral retraction & detumescence of lower third occur simultaneously & parallel rapidity of loss of erection in the male after ejaculation.)

CHART I (*Continued*)
The Sexual Response Cycle of the Human Female

Summary of Data from Masters, and Masters and Johnson (45–51).

	PHASE I. EXCITEMENT Duration: Several minutes to hours.	PHASE II. PLATEAU Duration: 30 seconds to 3 minutes.
GREATER VESTIBULAR GLANDS	No Change. (Phase II secretion may appear late in Phase I.)	A few drops of mucoid secretion (insufficient to lubricate vagina). Lubricates vestibule.
VAGINA	*DILATION & CONGESTION OF CIRCUM-VAGINAL PLEXI. Transudate-like Fluid.* First arousal sign appearing 10–30 sec. after any stimulation begins. Drops of clear fluid on vaginal wall; coalesce to form a well-lubricated vaginal barrel. (Aids in buffering acid vagina to neutral pH needed for sperm viability.) *Color Change.* Mucosa turns a patchy purplish color.	Copious transudate continues to form. (The more prolonged stimulation is before orgasm the more the transudate. No relationship between transudate & intensity of arousal; only factor is duration of stimulation, regardless of source—and time during menstrual cycle stimulation occurs: more is formed during the luteal phase.) *Color Change.* Becomes a uniform dark purple.
. . . **UPPER ⅔'s**	Dilates with convulsive, irregular movements as uterus moves up into false pelvis carrying anterior vaginal wall with it. Posterior fornices lengthen & vaginal rugae flatten out. Walls become thinner as vagina balloons out.	Further ballooning of upper vagina to a diameter of 2½–3 inches; then widens further as it relaxes in a slow, tensionless, irregular manner.
. . . **LOWER ⅓rd**	Modest dilation of vaginal lumen to 1–1¼ inches. Beginning congestion of walls.	Maximum congestion. Bulbs, labia minora & venous plexi reach maximum distention. Reduces vaginal lumen (of lower third) ½ or more size, creating gripping sensation on penis. Thrusts stimulate mucosa of lower third, labia & clitoris giving final surge of tension culminating in orgasm.
UTERUS	Moves up & back into lower abdomen late in Phase I. Exact cause unknown; possibly due to the massive venous congestion elevating pelvic floor (see text). (Elevation restricted or prevented with severe degrees of uterine retroversion interfering with full ballooning of upper ⅔'s of vagina.) *CERVIX.* Passively lifted up by uterine movement. No evidence of secretory activity during entire cycle.	*Contractions.* Strong contractions recorded beginning late in Phase II. They last up to 2+ minutes. Peristaltic motion runs from fundus, stopping at lower uterine segment. *CERVIX.* Slight swelling & patchy purplish color (inconstant; most apt to occur in multipara with chronic cervical infections).
PERINEAL BODY, RECTUM, and OTHERS	*FOURCHETTE.* Color changes during cycle as in labia minora.	*PERINEAL BODY.* Spasmodic tightening with involuntary elevations of perineum (reduced in multipara with poorly repaired obstetrical damage). Hyperventilation & carpopedal spasms usually present (the latter only with female-supine position).

PHASE III. ORGASM Duration: 3–15 seconds.	PHASE IV. RESOLUTION Duration: with orgasm, 10–25 minutes; with no orgasm, several hours
No Change.	No Change.
Transudate: Has produced maximum degree of lubrication.	Small amount of transudate collects on floor of the upper ⅔'s formed by its posterior wall (in supine position). Normally, ejaculate is deposited in this area forming a seminal pool.
- - - - - - - - No Change. (Walls fully ballooned out and motionless.) - - - - - - - - - 3–15 CONTRACTIONS: of lower third & upper portion of labia minora at ⅘ths sec. intervals. Strength depends on degree of venous congestion & pelvic muscle strength. First 5–6 contractions strongest.	- - - - - - - - Anterior wall slowly descends to rest against posterior wall (3–4 minutes), immersing cervix in seminal pool. Color & rugael pattern revert to normal in 10–15 min. or faster with orgasm. - - - - - - - - Swelling of walls disappears as rapidly as the loss of erection in the male after ejaculation. (If no orgasm, congestion persists for 20–30 minutes.)
Contractions continue throughout the orgasm. (They are particularly strong during pregnancy and are usually *stronger* during orgasm with masturbation than with coitus.)	Slowly returns to normal size dropping tip of cervix into seminal pool. *CERVIX:* Slight patulousness of external os in nullipara lasting 5–10 minutes. Normal size & color regained in same time it takes cervix to descend (up to 4 minutes).
PERINEAL BODY: Spasmodic constrictions (absent with obstet. damage). *RECTUM:* Rhythmical contractions (inconstant); more apt to occur in masturbation than coitus. *EXTERNAL URETHRAL SPHINCTER:* occasional contractions; no urine loss.	

the tissue spaces. So rapidly does this fluid pass through and edema occur that the *first* discernible sign of arousal is the appearance of droplets on the vaginal wall *within thirty seconds* from the moment stimulation begins. As the initially collapsed vaginal walls expand, the droplets coalesce, forming a well-lubricated vaginal barrel. In the upright position, the fluid begins flowing into the vestibule within a few minutes; in the supine position, its appearance will be slightly delayed. The rapid appearance of this fluid makes it similar (but not homologous) to the rapid appearance of the erection in men. This transudate, or fluid, is the chief, if not the only, source of vaginal lubrication (cervical secretions are absent, and greater vestibular glands secretions negligible). The vaginal transudate appears just rapidly with effective psychological stimulation alone.

Masters states (42, p. 65): ". . . this transudatelike material is the result of a marked dilation of the venous plexus concentration which encircles the entire barrel of the vagina. The bulbus vestibule, plexus pudendalis, plexus utero-vaginalis and, questionably, the plexus vesicalis and plexus hemorrhoidalis externus are all involved in a fulminating vasocongestive reaction along the walls of the vagina." The precise nature of this fluid has not been determined. It has the quality of a clear serous fluid with a slight mucoid consistency of unknown origin. (For brevity, I shall refer to this fluid as the vaginal transudate with the understanding that the exact mechanism of its production across the venous and vaginal walls and its consistency are still unknown.)

The quantity of transudation into the vagina may be taken as a measure of the quantity of transudation across all the venous plexi of the pelvis into the tissue spaces: an extraordinary massive fluid transfer must take place in a matter of minutes.

During the plateau phase, the total pelvic venous congestion and edema create a broad "platform" of distended tissues; especially involved are the lower third of the vagina, the vestibular bulbs, the labia minora—and labia majora in women who have borne several offspring—anterior commissure, and the uterus. In short, pelvic sexual tension is purely a vascular phenomenon of venous congestion and edema induced by effective stimulation of any erotogenic zone, physical or psychological.

Of special interest are the observations on two young women with surgically reconstructed artificial vaginas (45). In one, skin from the abdomen, and in the other, from the thigh, were grafted in forming the vaginal barrel. In both patients, one within two and a half, and the other, four months postoperatively, the vaginal transudate was appearing in a normal fashion through the new vaginal walls in quantities sufficient for coitus without additional lubrication.* This must mean that the venous plexi, either from the surgically traumatized circumvaginal area or from the bulbar-pudendal plexus (or both), had rapidly regenerated, grown upward, and positioned themselves with amazing purposefulness around the newly constructed vaginal barrel. Furthermore, during the same period, the skin grafts lost all their skin structures, taking on the exact cytology, gross and microscopic, of a normal vagina. The new mucous membrane was soon competently responding to sexual hormones with cyclic cornification and mucification. Within three and six months, respectively, both patients were experiencing regular vaginal orgasms during coitus, with the vagina and circumvaginal veins reacting as in normal women.

* Incidentally, both patients married shortly before their operations; and both husbands cooperated in the therapeutic program fully and intelligently. Their contribution to the highly successful outcomes cannot be overestimated.

The full implications of this spectacular ability of *the circumvaginal and bulbar veins and tissues* to induce structural regeneration, cellular transformation, and the creation of specialized venous networks capable of responding to hormones and to sexual stimulation will be developed at a later time. It is stressed now because this remarkable regenerative performance affirms the importance of the circumvaginal veins for sexual functioning: it is untenable to believe that such morphogenetic priority would be given to these structures without their functioning being of vital importance to the reproductive process.

3. Cause of the Orgasm

As in men, when the vasocongestive distension reaches a certain point, a reflex stretch mechanism in the responding muscles is set off, causing them to contract vigorously. These contractions expel the blood trapped in the tissue and venous plexi, creating the orgasmic sensations. The muscles of primary response (without which only the weakest orgasm could occur unless and until compensatory overgrowth of the remaining muscles could substitute) are: *the bilateral bulbocavernosi, transverse perineals, external anal sphincter, and rectus abdominus.* The muscles of secondary response and importance are: *the levator ani and the ischiocavernosi* (Figs. 3 and 4).

These are exactly the same muscles producing the orgasm and ejaculation in the male. Masters states (42, p. 71; 47, p. 90): ". . . the female responds to sexual stimulation . . . in a manner essentially akin to the localized congestive reaction which accomplishes erection in the male penis. . . . [And] actual orgasmic experiences are initiated in both sexes by similar muscle components."

4. The Sexual Cycle in Men

At this point, it will facilitate the presentation to interpose the observations Masters and Johnson (47) made on the sexual cycles of a series of 115 men (ages: 20–42 years). Only the data most relevant to the present theses are included.

a. The response cycle in men may be divided into the same four phases as in women, although they are less well defined.

b. Phase I is ushered in by the erection which occurs very rapidly (3 to 5 seconds) after the onset of effective stimulation. Phase I is short-lived compared to its duration in women and can be prolonged only by the deliberate use of delaying techniques. If such techniques are used, partial tumescence and detumescence may occur many times.

c. Phase I tumescence is accomplished primarily by the filling of the venous erectile bodies of the corpora cavernosi of the shaft. Phase II tumescence is achieved by the complete filling of the sinus-like cavities of the penile bulb, corpus spongiosum, and glans.

d. Late in Phase I, one third of all subjects show nipple erection. No tumescence of the areolae or breast tissues occurs. During resolution, up to one hour is required for nipple detumescence.

e. The sexual flush is identical in males and females, as is the sweating phenomenon during resolution, except that it occurs in 75 per cent of women and 25 per cent of men. (I suggest that the presence of the flush in only the very fair-skinned raises interesting questions about the relationship of skin vascularization and its response to the sexual hormones [skin erotism] and to melanin pigmentation.)

f. In Phase I, the most inconsequential psychosensory distractions easily impair the erection in all subjects regardless of how well acclimatized they are to the surroundings. (Analogous distractibility is not present in women.) In Phases II and III, sensory receptivity is markedly dulled.

g. Tightening of the scrotum and elevation of the testes against the perineum occur regularly, beginning in Phase I. The scrotum tenses and is elevated due to contraction of the

Dartos tunic and thickens due to vasocongestion. The testes increase somewhat in size from congestion and are elevated by contraction of the cremasteric muscles in the spermatic cords and by the congested scrotal floor. The testes, especially the left one, reach the perineum late in Phase II.

h. The distinctive sign of an impending orgasm (comparable to the color change of the labia minora in women) is a rapid, obvious increase in the size of the penile bulb and the corona glandis, which are the proximal and distal expansions of the corpus spongiosum. This occurs late in Phase II.

i. The ejaculation occurs in two stages. The first is produced by the slight contractions of the accessory organs, including the entire length of the vas, seminal vesicles, and prostate gland; this stage lasts only two to three seconds and gives the sensation of the inevitability of the oncoming orgasm.

Stage 2 is the ejaculation as commonly conceived. The semen is propelled through the penile urethra by the contractions of the responding muscles against the distended penile bulb. These are the same muscles producing the orgasm in the female with the addition of the constrictor muscles. (The urethra itself becomes congested, reaching two to three times its resting diameter.)

j. The initial three to four contractions of the ejaculation are the most pleasurable and powerful, depositing the major portion of the semen deep within the vagina. The initial contractions are followed by several minor ones with little expulsive force.

k. The rhythm of the first three to four contractions is always the same and identical to the rhythm of the contracting muscles in the female ($\frac{4}{5}$ second intervals); the minor contractions are more irregular.

l. Once the ejaculation starts, the contractions will continue involuntarily, whether or not stimulation continues.

(In females, orgasmic contractions will stop at any point if stimulation stops.)

m. Immediately upon completion of the ejaculation, the penile bulb shrinks in size *before any loss of tumescence in the corpora cavernosum of the shaft occurs.*

n. Detumescence occurs in two stages: the first is rapid, resulting in a partial involution of the erection and a refractory period during which restimulation cannot induce a second full erection. The second stage completes the involution and may be prolonged many minutes, especially if the penis is not withdrawn.

o. In some men, if the ejaculation is purposively restrained to create a prolonged excitement phase of intravaginal containment, the first-stage detumescence may be delayed for half an hour or more. (The authors have no explanation for this phenomenon at present.)

p. Many young men are capable of repetitive ejaculations. After the initial one, the erectile chambers return to a plateau-level refractory period. Within a few minutes, the bulbar chambers refill, and a full erection is regained. In one subject, the highest frequency of ejaculations was three within a ten-minute period from the onset of effective stimulation. The capacity for multiple orgasms is generally lost around the age of thirty. (Multiple ejaculations are different from recurrent cycles. In the latter, full detumescence and resolution occur with about a half-hour time lapse before restimulation effects another erection. In multiple orgasms, the sexual structures do not fall much below a plateau-phase congestion regardless of the strength of the orgasmic contractions.)

The foregoing data support an important conclusion. Points h, m, and n indicate that bulbar congestion produces the final surge of distension necessary to effect both an orgasm and its intensity. Furthermore, first-stage detumescence is produced by the emptying of the bulb alone, with the corpora cavernosum serving only to create and maintain the erection. Once the ejaculation is complete, the shaft erectile sinus-like cavities begin to empty. (This is to be expected since there are no muscle fibers in the shaft, except the constrictors in the urethra and a prolongation of the Dartos tunic* in the more loosely organized tissue beneath the surface. The large responding muscles producing the ejaculation insert only into the most proximal end of the corpora fascia.)

Therefore the penile shaft actually does not participate in the ejaculatory response to any appreciable extent; the more gradual emptying of the shaft tissue would then comprise much of the second-stage detumescence.† (This corresponds to the comparable condition in the female where clitoral corpora and glans do not participate in the orgasm.) Moreover, the importance of the bulbar contractions explains why men suffering from penile amputation and women from clitoral amputations are capable of experiencing orgasms so long as the bulbs are intact. Hence in both sexes the corpora and the glans belong primarily in the category of the erotogenic resources of the body rather than with the structures of direct orgasmic response.

---

* The thin layer of scattered muscle tissue on the skin of the scrotum. A similar layer is found in the skin of the labia majora.

† The lack of participation of the corpora cavernosum of the shaft in the orgasmic response correlates with the more uniform size of these structures compared to the bulb, mentioned earlier. A similar uniformity of vaginal expansion occurs in women (see p. 88). Here is an interesting example of selective pressure at work. The length of the penis is important only for the proper deposition of semen, not for the orgasm itself. Thus the penile length and vaginal expansion have become increasingly uniform, to match each other, i.e., increasingly separated from genetic variability. However, by remaining of variable sizes, the penile bulb is subjected to selective pressure, allowing the breeding success to go to the males with the greatest bulbar capacity for sexual tension and ejaculatory force. The same considerations would apply to the vestibular bulbs in the female.

5. Duration of the Orgasm

As a general rule, a woman's orgasm lasts about twice as long as a man's in so far as the effective contractions are concerned. The overall duration is about the same. In men, there are three to four very strong contractions that deposit most of the semen; these are followed by numerous irregular, minor contractions. In women, the orgasm consists of eight to fifteen muscular contractions, of which the first five to six or more are of the ⅘ second rhythm and the most intense. Hence the first-stage, most forceful and pleasurable contractions have an average duration of about three to four seconds in the male and five to six seconds in the female.

6. Intensity of the Orgasm in Both Sexes

Naturally it is most difficult to judge the intensity of the initial major muscle contractions in males and females. It is an age-old belief that men generally experience more intense orgasms than women. However, Masters and Johnson's description of the bodily reactions and emotional responses of women during the orgasm indicates that the difference is not very great *if* the woman has a fully developed orgasmic "platform" of widely distended veins and tissues. The explanation of the existing difference lies in two factors. First, there is a much greater generalized vasocongestion and edema of the woman's entire pelvic area compared to the more localized congestion in the male. With all venous plexi and bulbs maximally distended, the total blood volume to be removed by the muscle contractions is simply greater in the female. Secondly, orgasmic intensity is a function of the strength of the contracting muscles. A difference due to the greater size and strength of the pelvic muscles in men is to be expected. However, excepting extreme differences in body size and muscle mass, this size differential is mitigated by the greater size of the female's pelvic outlet. The outlet, spanned by the muscles of orgasmic response, is absolutely longer in all diameters in the female than in the male.

It would seem that the male expends much of the strength of the muscles' contractile force during the first three to four contractions as an adaptive device which insures the deposition of semen deep in the vaginal barrel. With no such function required of the female, the initial contractions need not be so intense. Hence, the female's orgasm can be more prolonged, which is a nice adaptive device insuring the expulsion of the greatest amount of pelvic vascular congestion.

I would stress the importance of the removal of the massive pelvic congestion, especially in those women experiencing frequent coition who have borne children. With venous congestion and dilated veins the inevitable by-products of pregnancy, chronic pelvic congestion furthered by inadequate or absent orgasmic release fosters a pelvic condition conducive to many disorders interfering with impregnation, pregnancies, and general health (59, p. 472).

Therefore, I propose that throughout primate evolution selective pressure has always tended in the direction of favoring the development of the longer duration of the intense orgasmic contractions in the females and the shorter, more intense contractions in the male. In general, the orgasm in the male is admirably designed to deposit the semen where it will do the most good, and in the female, to remove the largest amount of venous congestion in the most effective manner.

7. Clitoral Retraction and the Preputial-Glandar Mechanism

One of the most significant findings of Masters and Johnson is that the clitoral glans is kept in a state of continuous stimulation throughout intravaginal coition even though it is apparently not being touched and appears to have vanished.

Clitoral erection causes the shaft to retract into the swollen prepuce or clitoral hood and occurs in every woman, regardless of the type of stimulation, coital position, degree of clitoral tumescence or the initial clitoral size (Fig. 7). This phenomenon occurs much later than the homologous erection in the male, approximately one and a half to three minutes before the orgasm. Retraction occurs whether or not the clitoral area is stimulated during Phases I and II, although it generally takes place a minute or so sooner with prior clitoral-area manipulation than without it.

Masters and Johnson stress that retraction removes the clitoris from the vaginal orifice even further, making penile contact all the more impossible. They state (46, p. 253):

> A mechanical traction develops on both sides of the clitoral hood subsequent to penile distension of the vaginal outlet. With penile thrusts, the entire clitoral body is pulled towards the pudendum by traction exerted on the wings of the minor labial hood.
>
> When the penile shaft is withdrawn during active coition, traction on the clitoral hood is somewhat relieved and the body and glans return to the normal pudendal overhang positioning. . . . This rhythmic movement of the clitoral body in conjunction with intravaginal thrusting and withdrawal of the penis develops significant secondary sexual tension levels. It should be emphasized that this same type of secondary clitoral stimulation occurs in every coital position, when there is full penetration of the vaginal barrel by the erect penis.

Clitoral retraction is accomplished by the ischiocavernosi muscles (which contract, contrary to their lengthening in men to allow erection), distension of the crura, and shortening of the suspensory ligament via its attachment to the rectus abdominus. In men, the erection initiates the cycle and is

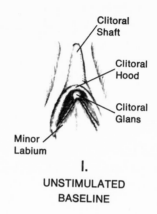

I.

UNSTIMULATED
BASELINE

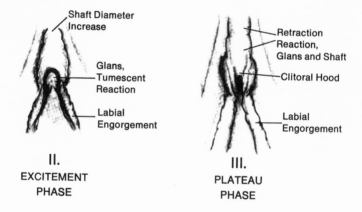

II.

EXCITEMENT
PHASE

III.

PLATEAU
PHASE

Figure 7. Retraction of the clitoris. From Masters and Johnson, "The Sexual Response Cycle of the Human Female. III. The Clitoris: Anatomic and Clinical Considerations." *Western Journal of Surgery, Obstetrics & Gynecology.* (46) Reproduced in *Human Sexual Response*, Boston: Little, Brown, 1966.

produced probably only by vasocongestion by virtue of the sudden expansion of the corpora at the right-angle bend at the lower border of the symphysis. In women, the homologous erection occurs often fifteen to twenty minutes later than the male's, and the minimal degree of clitoral shaft tumescence could not produce similar straightening. Hence the action of the ischiocavernosi muscles is required. (Since the clitorial shaft is held in retraction by muscle force and not tumescence, the lack of shaft movement during the orgasm presents an additional puzzle. Probably the combined action of the ischiocavernosi and bulbocavernosi fibers to the shaft [Fig. 4] operates in some fashion so as to prevent shaft movement.)

Preputial-Glandar Action—The difference in the action of the ischiocavernosi in men and women is an interesting example of sexual dimorphism and, I think, significant for several reasons. In men, the vascular sinusoids of the shaft hold a prodigious quantity of blood during erection. One might think the clitoral corpora would also hold a large quantity of blood relative to their size. However, since the contraction of the ischiocavernosi is required to pull the shaft up onto the anterior symphyseal border, this same action flattens the shaft against the pubic symphysis, thus precluding the possibility of the shaft holding an appreciable quantity of blood. (In all women, the shaft diameter increases, but it rarely lengthens. The glans always swells, but in only 50 per cent is this grossly visible.) The corpora sinusoids dilate with arousal; however, the backward pull of the ischiocavernosi forces the distended sinusoids to spread only laterally. Hence increases in shaft diameter are universal, and lengthening is rare. Of course, engorgement of the cryptic crura is necessary to stretch the ischiocavernosi, so that this engorgement must proceed during Phase I.

As the primate study will show, the preputial-glandar mechanism has evolved some extraordinary anatomical patterns, all designed with one purpose: to insure that the glans is maximally stimulated by the swollen prepuce during thrusting movements. Referring to Figure 6, I would suggest a fact about the preputial-glandar mechanism not heretofore appreciated. In both women and most primates, thrusting movements produce two actions on the glans: the prepuce is pulled over the glans and the shaft is pulled partially out of retraction. The former is the primary source of glandar friction, the latter is the secondary source. The importance of this latter action in all primates remains to be determined. Unlike the penis, the human clitoris is not pendulous. At rest, it is sharply retroflexed posteriorly, with the degree of retroflexion varying in different women. In men, erection elevates the penis through a 90° arc; in women, the clitoral shaft is moved through approximately a 180° arc or somewhat less. (Actually the tip of the glans traces an elliptical curve forward, since retraction occurs with an almost violent and sudden foreshortening or telescoping of the shaft, so that it assumes a cone shape [41].) Thus clitoral retroflexion allows the glans to be moved a longer distance back and forth by penile thrusting. It would seem that the crural system is given over almost entirely to the preputial-glandar mechanism; therefore the bulbs and anterior commissure (i.e., the components encircling the vaginal orifice) are the only clitoral structures left to become distended and to participate in the orgasmic discharge.

I submit that the same preputial-glandar action will be found to exist in most, if not all, the primates. Moreover, the fantastic variations in the glans-preputial-labial anatomy, all with the purpose of maintaining or improving the frictional action of the glans against the inner layer of the preputial mucous membrane, are impressive evidence of the extent to which evolution has gone to perfect this mechanism. Its importance to the successful performance of the sexual act seems undeniable.

Masters and Johnson have shown that repeated relaxations and retractions of the shaft take place, equal in number to the number of thrusting movements. Consequently
the more the thrusting, the more the erotic arousal in the
woman. To this I would add: the greater the swelling of the
prepuce, the closer it will envelop the glans as it moves back
and forth or as the prepuce is pulled over the glans. The
greater the retraction of the shaft, the greater will be the
distance through which the glans moves during thrusting.
The greater the labial swelling, the tighter the prepuce will
be over the glans and the better the traction. Therefore, only
if the clitoral shaft does *not* retract and seemingly disappear,
due to inadequate stimulation, is it removed from participation in the erotogenic build-up.

It is now clear why so few women (or primates) employ
digital stimulation of the lower vagina during masturbation
or prefer it during foreplay as a primary source of arousal.
The glans has a much higher erotogenic potential than does
the mucous membrane of the lower third (p. 118); moreover, considerable distension of the vaginal orifice must occur before traction on the labia can be effective. The fingers
cannot substitute for the erect penis in this action.

Furthermore, it is also obvious why the thrusting movements of the penis will necessarily create simultaneous stimulation of the lower third of the vagina, labia minora, and
clitoral shaft and glans as an integrated, inseparable functioning unit, with the glans being the most important and, in
by far the majority of instances, the indispensable initiator
of the orgasmic reaction. With these observations, the evidence seems overwhelming: *it is a physical impossibility to
separate the clitoral from the vaginal orgasm as demanded
by psychoanalytic theory.**

---

* The preputial-glandar mechanism clarifies the question of the orgasm
in all female mammals performing coitus in the ventrodorsal position,
indicating that dorsal entry does not rule out effective clitoral stimula-

(This new fact creates problems in terminology. There is a vast difference between clitoral stimulation to induce orgasm by digital stimulation alone and clitoral stimulation culminating in orgasm by intravaginal thrusting. The term "vaginal orgasm" is perfectly permissible as long as it is understood that the thrusting is effective because it stimulates the clitoris. No doubt such understanding will not be universal, and the confusion will remain for many years to come.)

The sharp distinction in the value of the prepuce for the male and female is, I propose, of signal importance. Circumcision exposes the glans, making it less sensitive to tactile stimulation; thus the circumcised man can generally hold an erection longer because the slightly insensitive glans requires more vigorous stimulation. The uncircumcised man may be stimulated to ejaculation more quickly, but the glans is more sensitive, so that multiple or repetitive orgasms are somewhat easier to achieve. In neither case is the prepuce essential to the man's performance. Strangely enough, *with clitoral retraction, the female actually uses the swollen preputial sac in the same manner the male uses the vaginal barrel to achieve stimulation of the penis.* Functionally speaking, the clitoral hood is a miniature vagina.

Women almost always require a prolonged Phase I which the uncircumcised man often has more or less difficulty achieving. The relationship that this fact bears to the fairly sudden and widespread adoption of circumcision among so many early Neolithic peoples provides some interesting speculations which are beyond the scope of this book.

---

tion, as tentatively hypothesized by Ford and Beach (15, p. 30). A well-developed prepuce and highly distensible labia minora occur in almost every species. The exceptions are so few and occur in animals so inadequately studied, especially during heat, that for the moment we may consider this anatomy and its functioning to be a universal mammalian female characteristic.

Nevertheless, two points are sufficiently germane to warrant mention. First, in several of the African primates, the prepuce in the male is short, permanently retracted. Nature has performed her own circumcision, as it were. Secondly, there is mounting evidence that matriarchal-like cultures did, in fact, exist in the ancient Near East and northern Africa until or near the beginning of historic times. It seems probable that the simplest explanation for the origin of the idea of circumcision would be that the peoples observed these animals and saw the more prolonged copulations they would be able to achieve. The introduction of the idea into human customs may have come first from the women during early Mesolithic times; however, the men must have shown considerable resistance to such a barbaric act of symbolic castration which, as initially practiced, must have taken its toll in actual castration and in lives through infections and blood poisoning (especially since it was first performed on pubertal boys). It was probably practiced regularly only in the centers where the women wielded unusual power. The real force behind the widespread implementation of the idea would have arisen with the growth of agriculture and the rise of the patriarchal societies where polygyny so universally replaced polyandry or whatever types of social structure in prior existence. Polygyny without circumcision would be difficult, if not impossible, to maintain in a society in which the women expected and demanded to experience frequent and regular orgasmic satisfaction. Here, as elsewhere, economic advantage could have advanced this most inhumane practice quickly and then incorporated it into divine law.

8. The Upper Two-Thirds of the Vagina

The upper portion of the vaginal wall is the only part of the genital tract (excepting the possibility of the still-unstudied ovaries and tubes) which does not respond to sexual stimulation with intense vasocongestion and edema. It plays no role in either erotogenesis or orgasmic action. Even the ballooning out of the upper two thirds is accomplished by the upward movement of the uterus carrying the cervix and anterior vaginal wall with it. This action is fairly well completed during Phase I; thereafter the upper two thirds remains relaxed, thinned down, ballooned out, and motionless for the remainder of the plateau and orgasmic phases. This upper vaginal ballooning invariably occurs with effective arousal, regardless of the stimulative source. The motionlessness precludes the possibility of the upper vagina participating in the orgasm. It also precludes the possibility of the upper vagina stimulating the penile shaft; it does not touch the penis except where the glans contacts the most cranial end of the vaginal barrel. Vaginal diameter at the point of maximal ballooning is about 3 inches; and this is a surprisingly uniform measurement in all women, regardless of body size or intensity of arousal (44).

During embryogenesis, immediately after that point in time when male differentiation is complete, the vagina of the genetic female begins to form as an upward proliferation of solid cells from the urogenital sinus. Its full growth and canalization requires three more months (11). The vagina is, indeed, a unique female possession, well constructed to be a penile-semen receptacle and birth canal, but not to participate in the creation or release of sexual tension.

Descent of the Cervix—The purpose of the motionless upper two thirds is shown in Figure 8. In the supine position, the sagging posterior vaginal wall becomes its floor into which drains some of the transudate. With ejaculation, seminal fluid is deposited into this pool, and buffering action from the transudate protects the sperm from the acid vaginal fluids. With orgasms, the generalized pelvic venous congestion is relieved; the anterior wall of the vagina and the cervix descend together until the tip of the cervix is immersed in the seminal pool.

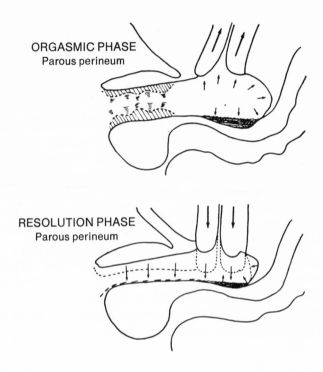

Figure 8. **The orgasmic and resolution phases of the female sexual response cycle, showing contractions of the lower third of the vagina during the orgasm and the descent of the cervix during resolution.** From Masters and Johnson, "The Sexual Response Cycle of the Human Male." *Western Journal of Surgery, Obstetrics & Gynecology.* (47) Reproduced in *Human Sexual Response,* Boston: Little, Brown, 1966.

Masters (41) states their research team has data showing there is no sucking action by the uterus through the cervix.* Hence, there is no evidence to date that the sperm ascend the cervical canal by any mechanism other than their own motility. The authors have also demonstrated how damaged and malpositioned pelvic structures can interfere with conception by interfering with cervical descent.

Since full cervical descent can be achieved normally only with the woman lying in the supine position during the postorgasmic three to four minutes required for descent, I suggest that this mode of insemination must be another uniquely human adaptation.

9. The Lower Third of the Vagina and the Labia Minora

Understanding the changes in the lower third is most important, since so much erroneous functioning has been attributed to this structure. The action of the labia minora in the preputial-glandar mechanism has been discussed; their functioning in conjunction with the lower third is taken up here.

The Lower Third as an Erotogenic Zone—Masters and Johnson consider the lower third to constitute an erotogenic zone during active thrusting equal to that of the clitoral shaft, although neither has the exquisite sensitivity of the glans. I suggest the sensitivity of the lower third and the

---

* Heiman (23) drew his conclusions from the theory of the existence of the cervical sucking action before this work was done. He also posited some truth to the notion that a woman is more apt to become pregnant if she has a strong orgasm because of the presumed sucking action. Actually, Masters states that the penis is frequently withdrawn before cervical immersion is completed (three to four minutes). In a woman with a lax perineal body who has borne children, semen easily escapes with premature withdrawal, whereas if the woman does *not* have an orgasm, the still-swollen lower third acts as a stopper to semen outflow. In this connection of the relation of orgasm to impregnation, the proven existence of reflex ovulation in a few women (57, p. 134) seems to me to be of more than passing interest.

labia minora is about equal, since these two areas have the same embryological origin and function as a unit during arousal.

The entire vagina is literally enveloped in a layer of anastomosing* veins, especially thick around the lower third where the bulbar-pudendal and vaginal plexi merge. During Phase I, the vaginal canal dilates to 1 to 1¼ inches as the result of the ballooning of the upper two thirds. With Phase II congestion, the engorged venous sheath with the bulbs press the vaginal walls inward, narrowing the vaginal lumen to less than 50 per cent of its diameter during Phase I. This narrowing of the lumen creates the gripping sensation felt on the penile shaft.

Thus the tightening of the vaginal walls around the penile shaft permits highly effective frictional stimulation to be applied to the shaft by the lower third and, reciprocally, to the lower third by the shaft, thereby significantly elevating the sexual tension level, often to orgasmic intensity, in both partners. It is now apparent that the greater the distension of veins and bulbs, the greater the pressure on the penis, on the lower third, the upper labia, and the clitoral glans via the labial-preputial mechanism. All operate as a well-coordinated unit.

The very sensitive labia minora contribute much to the erotogenicity of the lower third in that they add up to ¾ inch of functional sidewalls to the vaginal length. Much of the stimulative force many women locate at the mouth of the vagina may stem from the upper labia. The distal labial folds become swollen and evert, as in most female mammals, creating a well-lubricated vestibular funnel which directs the penis into the vaginal orifice.

The Lower Third in the Orgasmic Response—The muscular layer of the lower vaginal wall is thin and composed mainly of longitudinally disposed fibers with a few inter-
* See glossary.

spersed circularly disposed fibers. Whatever intrinsic contracting value these fibers might have would be counteracted by this arrangement, since longitudinal fiber contractions would shorten the vaginal barrel (it is lengthened by $1\frac{1}{2}$ to 2 inches or more). In answer to my question on the importance of the vaginal wall musculature compared to the extravaginal muscles in producing the orgasm, Masters states (41): "I would expect some minor degree of orgasmic platform contraction, even after removal of the transverse perineal muscles and a total vulvectomy. However, I would be completely amazed if the intensity of the reaction were to be that recordable in the undamaged state."

The musculature of the pelvic floor surrounding the lower third (Figs. 3 and 4) contract rhythmically against the engorged venous plexi and bulbs, forcing out the blood trapped in them, thus creating the orgasm. (This means that the responding muscles must possess a special stretch mechanism, but the precise nature of the neurophysiological control of these contractions is not known.) The contractions cause the lower third, upper labia, and bulbs to contract forcibly. It must be stressed that the contractions develop just as forcibly with any type of sexual arousal or coital position and whether or not there is anything for the lower third to contract against. During intercourse the contractions can be felt on the penile shaft, sometimes described as "snapping sensations."

The authors have yet to study the changes of the vestibular bulbs during arousal; they are not open to inspection. However, the bulbar plexus is so intimately related to the lower vaginal plexus that it is impossible to separate these expandable containers of venous blood. The importance of the bulbs is obvious from their huge size compared to the rest of the clitoral complex, their extreme distensibility with arousal, and their strategic positioning around the lower third.

The Color Change—A related phenomenon of interest is the very sudden Phase II color change of the labia minora —to a brilliant red in women who have never borne children and burgundy red in those who have—which always heralds an oncoming orgasm within three minutes or less if stimulation is continued. No explanation of this reaction is given.* Since the abrupt color change is so strictly limited to the labia, is indicative of the coming orgasm, and is homologous to the preorgasmic, full distension of the penile bulb and corona glandis in men, one wonders what homologous venous networks and hormonal action might mediate this color change. Four events—the onset of clitoral retraction, narrowing of the vaginal lumen, firmness of the upper labia, and the color change—all occur at the same time. It is reasonable to assume that they are related reactions. A detailed study of the neurophysiological changes involved in these reactions and their homologues in men should be rewarding, since it is precisely at this point, the color change ushering in the plateau phase, where so many sexual cycles in women fail.

The data thus far permit two important conclusions:

(i) The mucous membrane lining the lower third of the vagina is an erotogenic zone during the thrusting action in coitus, with an unknown degree of sensitivity (see Chapter 4). However, *no part of the vagina itself produces the orgasmic contractions.* The muscular contractions engender-

* Masters and Johnson call attention to the similarity of the color change and the "sexual skin" of rhesus. It might be noted that there is no exact physiological similarity. The skin vasodilation of the mature rhesus is present at all times in females and, to a lesser degree, in males. In females, it covers the lower abdomen, perineum, inner thighs to the knees, the circumnipple area, and the face. It is always a bright Mercurochrome-red. It becomes more extensive and brilliant throughout estrus (and during sexual arousal in males) but does not turn burgundy-venous red (26). Whether or not the portion of the sexual skin limited to the labia turns an even deeper red just prior to an orgasm has yet to be looked for.

ing the actual sensation of orgasm are produced by the extravaginal muscles contracting, not against the vaginal wall directly but against the circumvaginal venous chambers. The lower vaginal wall is passively pushed in and out by these contractions.

Therefore there is no such thing as an orgasm of the vagina. What exists is an orgasm of the circumvaginal venous chambers. The actual apparatus for orgasmic production is the same in the female as in the male: contractions of the responding muscles against the erectile chambers in men produce expulsion of blood and, indirectly, of semen by compressing the urethra; in the female, contractions produce expulsion of blood and, indirectly, contractions of the lower vagina.

(ii) Men have three erectile bodies: two corpora cavernosi with their crura and one bulb with its shaft extension, the corpus spongiosum, carrying the urethra. The ejaculatory contractions compress the bulb, primarily, which presses on the urethra expelling the semen. The shaft sinusoids do not participate in the orgasm but maintain the erection throughout the process of semen expulsion.

Women have five erectile bodies. The two corpora cavernosi with their crura become engorged, but the quantity of blood contained is negligible compared to the male's. The two vestibular bulbs with their anterior commissure extension into the shaft are the second. The third is the large circumvaginal plexus into which drain all the veins of the perineum. Thus the vestibular bulbs and the circumvaginal plexus constitute the major erectile bodies of the female.

The physiological action of the vestibular bulbs is nicely harmonized with that of the circumvaginal plexus, a point which will necessitate a re-evaluation of the hormonal control of these structures.

The striking difference in the response of the upper and lower vagina (the upper wall thins out, relaxes and balloons;

the lower becomes congested, thickens and contracts) does not have any immediately perceivable hormonal or neural explanation. The difference must involve differing vascular permeability and muscle action. The two portions of the vagina clearly show different embryonic origins. Moreover, the clitoris is known to be very sensitive to androgens; yet the clitoral bulbs and their plexus respond in unison with the vaginal plexus, which is known to be very responsive to estrogens. The similarity of response of the bulbar apparatus and the circumvaginal veins forces considerations of the possibility that these structures are under the same hormonal control which is different from that of the crura, shaft, and glans. The embryonic origin of the bulbs at the same time as the vagina lends credence to this suggestion. Should these suppositions prove true, there is a good likelihood that a similar bihormonal control of the male bulb versus the shaft corpora, involving both androgens and estrogens, might exist; and our entire understanding of the hormonal control of sexuality will need revision.

These are only a few of the many ramifications of the Masters and Johnson research.

10. Uterus

The uterus regularly reacts with strong, slow contractions, probably induced by the vasocongestive process throughout the walls (61). Masters (41) now has data demonstrating that the uterine contractions have the same recorded pattern as those of the first stage of labor, differing only in amplitude. For this reason as well as the fact that women with hysterectomies experience orgasms with no decrease in intensity, these contractions would play no important role in orgasmic intensity. The cause and function of the uterine contractions are unknown.

I would suggest that these contractions may offer a clue to the postcoital nausea experienced by some women. This

has heretofore been considered psychogenic in origin, although many women with apparently good marital and sexual adjustments are often aware of postcoital nausea. With
the ligamentous attachments of the swollen uterus to the
dorsal peritoneum and with congestion of the ligaments
themselves, gastrointestinal functioning would be affected.

11. Sexual Arousal and the Luteal Phase of the Menstrual Cycle

It has been long realized that sexual arousal tends to occur
more readily during the luteal phase, or last 14 days, of the
menstrual cycle. Kinsey et al. (31) demonstrated this correlation statistically, indicating that roughly 90 per cent of
American women prefer relations during the luteal or premenstrual phase. Masters and Johnson have shown that the
patients with artificial vaginae, as well as normal women,
produce a more copious transudate with arousal during
this period indicating a greater vasocongestion and vascular
permeability. This circumstance plus the well-known fact of
the pelvic edema which builds up to a greater or lesser degree during the premenstrual phase in all women make it
clear that the increased sexual capacity is related to venous
congestion and edema.

As a generalization, only a very few of the 90 per cent of
women noted by Kinsey are unable to reach orgasms at all
during the follicular (ovulatory), or first 14 days, phase of
the cycle. (Probably all women can reach orgasm at this
time if adequately stimulated.) Rather, during the luteal
phase, the majority of women have a greater spontaneous
interest in sexual matters, experience a greater desire to ini-
tiate love-making, find an increased ease in reaching the
plateau phase of arousal, have a more copious transudate of
a different, slightly "slippery" consistency, and achieve multiple orgasms with greater ease. This facilitation of sexual
responsivity is due primarily to the higher base line of pelvic

congestion and edema characteristic of the premenstrual phase and, in part, to the increased influences in support of a possible pregnancy at this time.

These findings support the conclusion that the majority of women manifest *some degree of enhanced luteal-phase sexuality,* which means they are *maximally* potent only during the ten to fourteen days of the premenstrual period, i.e., about half the time. During the luteal phase, the base line of pelvic congestion becomes increasingly higher until one to two days before the menses when hormonal support is withdrawn and is finally relieved by the flow. (If the congestion is too great, the pain and discomfort will override the sensations of sexual tension.) The relief of tension or discomfort is often not apparent until the second day of the menses when the heaviest flow begins. (In clinical practice, I have known two patients who regularly engaged in coitus during the menses and reported their greatest sexual responsivity during the first two days.)

Because of the higher luteal base line of congestion, women are in a mild state of sexual excitement throughout this period, although it is rarely recognized as such. (This is a far cry, of course, from saying women experience "heat" during the premenstrual period. The term "heat" describes an estrus or follicular phase sexuality with an interestrus or non-heat phase of total nonresponsiveness.) Frequent and successful coitions temporarily relieve the discomfort of premenstrual tension. In women with strong sexual guilts, successful coitions are rarer, especially since they usually cannot admit the possibility of self-engendered, "automatic" sexual arousal; unrelieved sexual tension could then be a main component of the premenstrual tension syndrome.

Naturally, psychogenic factors can be so strong as to overcome all these physiological restrictions or mitigate them considerably, although certainly not all the time. In general, all further statements in this book concerning changes during the sexual cycle assume a well-developed state of pelvic congestion that is most apt to occur during the luteal phase of the menstrual cycle.

The following hypothesis can now be confirmed. The entire chain of events unfolding during each luteal phase (the increasing pelvic congestion, increased vaginal fluid and spontaneously generated interest) *is* homologous to the period of heat of certain higher primates. These mammals differ from all others in that they menstruate and that continuous *receptivity* is possible. Coition with penetration may occur between heats, but it is believed that females never experience sexual arousal or orgasm during these episodes. Certainly from all observations so far, this between-heat sexual *responsivity,* if present at all, is rare and would be a negligible factor in social life and evolutionary direction. The homology resides in the cyclicity of enhanced sexual drive due to recurring waves of hormonally induced pelvic congestion and edema.

In the primates, ovulatory congestion and edema are largely concentrated in the superficial perineal tissues. In women, luteal-phase congestion and edema have a more generalized distribution, but with the largest concentration in the uterus and its appendages; during sexual arousal in women, the congestion and edema become concentrated in the superficial perineal tissues. In both groups, the vascularizing, fluid-imbibing, growth-producing estrogens are probably the same.

It is important to realize that there is no essential physiological difference between heat or estrus cycles and menstrual cycles. The only new elements introduced by menstrual cycles are caused by a shifting of hormonal action and consist of (a) interestrus or continuous sexuality of a greater or lesser degree; and (b) the uterine build-up in preparation for a possible pregnancy so great the decidua cannot be resorbed whether or not the embryo implants; it must be shed (a good part of it is still resorbed).

Among the primates with their menstrual cycles, women show two significant differences caused by physiologically minor changes, which sociologically have had profound results. The first is the shift in the timing of hormonal action; hormones are produced constantly at physiologically active levels and elaborated in much greater quantities during the premenstrual build-up. I suggest that the key to understanding the human female's "escape from estrus" lies in the mechanism behind the release of the two or three fluid-imbibing estrogens from their rigidly limited activity during the first fourteen days of the menstrual cycle. The evolutionary demand for this estrogen release would have been great due to the increasing body size of the early humanoids and the lengthening pregnancies associated with increasing fetalization, or slowing of the growth of the embryo. The more vascularized and proliferated the uterus and placenta the better, especially since fetal loss due to the developing upright posture made uterine anchorage of vital importance.

Secondly, in all the higher primates but humans, estrus is completely suppressed during the first part of lactation. Lactation anestrus insures the infant his mother's undivided attention during his first six months. When estrus heats are re-established, the infant can shift for himself for long periods. (However, with the constant elaboration of large quantities of these estrogens and progestins, especially during pregnancies, the humanoid females were under stronger, constant hormonal pressure and so produced larger placentae, bigger babies, and heavier, longer milk flow.) A postpartum breakthrough in human females of these influences on the ovaries and uterus began to occur a few weeks after delivery. This resumption of sexuality while the newborn baby is still totally helpless is a human condition, not shared by other primates, which had profound effects on the social life of mankind. I suggest that lactation ovulation with reinstitution of the menstrual cycle was not particularly adaptive but an incidental by-product of the recently achieved disruption of the timing control of hormonal activity plus the enormous production of hormones that occurs in preparation for pregnancy throughout the reproductive tract and entire body. (It also accounts for the erotic arousal many women experience when nursing their infants, at times to the point of orgasm.)

Finally, to my knowledge, no one has followed through with a study on that other 10 per cent found by Kinsey. It seems possible that the 10 per cent of women who prefer intercourse during the ovulatory phase of their cycles may be those in whom the transition to enhanced sexuality during the last fourteen days has not yet occurred to its fullest extent. If so, we have a strong indication of how recently this second-phase hypersexuality must have evolved.

The entire subject of premenstrual tension, the hormonal changes mediating the shift from heat cycles to enhanced sexual arousal from about the fifteenth day in the cycle to the menses, and the adaptation pressures during evolution that brought it about will be elaborated later. The major implication of this hypothesis now, however, is to indicate the very great similarity in the sexual response cycles of women and many primates and the continued cyclicity of women's sexuality. Thus, on another score, the "wide" gap between women's sexuality and the animals' is nonexistent.

12. The Relationship of the Orgasm to Pregnancies
Many women experience their first coital orgasm after their first pregnancy. Heretofore the reason advanced has been psychological: lessening of anxiety and the maturing experience of a successful pregnancy, labor, and care of the newborn offspring. I would suggest that the beginning of

orgasmic competency after the first pregnancy has more to do with the greatly increased vascularity of the entire pelvis induced by the pregnancy hormones with the resultant growth of new blood vessels and of varicosities. An additional possibility is the effect of androgen and the androgenic action of progesterone, both of which are elaborated in huge quantities during pregnancy, on the responsivity of the clitoral system and the strength of the muscles of orgasmic response.

Masters and Johnson's observations add to our understanding of the seemingly paradoxical effects of the sexual hormones. Some women respond with more sexual drive to androgens and some to estrogens. Masters and M. H. Grady (43) demonstrated early the value of the use of both hormones in the treatment of women in the aging period; the present work gives further evidence of the rationale of their actions. Both the congestive-edema effect of estrogens and the muscular, orgasmic action of androgen are as essential to the sexual cycle of women as they both are in men. (In men, estrogens are produced by the testes and adrenals.) Where the female pelvis is already well vascularized or in a state of chronic congestion, estrogens would create more discomfort; whereas androgens would induce increased erotization of the clitoral complex and increase the contractile strength of the responding muscles. Where poor vascularization exists, androgens would not help.

In all women, so long as obstetrical damage does not intervene, pregnancies will increase the volume capacity of the pelvic venous bed, increase the volume of the sexual edema, enhance the capacity for sexual tension, and improve orgasmic intensity, frequency, and pleasure. I suggest that natural selection has taken advantage of every random opportunity to make enhanced sexual pleasure the insurance that motherhood will continue unabated.

13. Duration of the Excitement Stage

An apparent minor point deserves attention because of its importance to evolutionary biology and to human relationships. The period of time from the onset of effective stimulation to the plateau stage, i.e., Phase I or the foreplay period, may be prolonged for many hours. However, with experienced couples, particularly, it rarely is. Under ordinary circumstances, it is the man who will be forced to utilize the delaying techniques because it takes longer, as a rule, for the female to reach the plateau stage than the male. She cannot speed up her excitement stage by the use of any conscious techniques. Generally, the average time of the excitement stage for women, given uniformity of the usual variables (mood, fatigue, timing, etc.) will be approximately the same with any form of stimulation and will be, on average, longer than that of the male. The reason is that the female undergoes a more generalized pelvic vasocongestive process than the male, which simply takes longer to develop fully. Women have a larger volume capacity of venous networks to maintain in the engorged state, and they produce a much larger outflow of edema fluid from the vessels to the tissue spaces. This conclusion is substantiated by the fact that, with increasing sexual experience and childbirth, a woman's excitement phase does *not* lessen in duration because experience and childbirth increase the venous bed capacity.

In this connection, Masters and Johnson note an infrequent situation of psychological interest. If a couple are under unusually optimal conditions for arousal, physically and psychologically, the excitement phase in the man may progress to the plateau phase in no more than a minute or so; and in the woman, about twice as long. Under such circumstances, it is not unusual to find that the physiological processes have progressed to the point of full sexual readiness in both partners before either is consciously aware of any major degree of sexual tension at all. Full orgasms will then occur in both.

This observation seems to me to be a strong comment on two points: (a) Under circumstances most favorable for sexual expression, the participation of the higher cortical and intellectual centers in sexual arousal is nil. In therapy, it often seems as if we help our patients *to think* their way into achieving an orgasm or a "vaginal" orgasm (see footnote on p. 22). In reality we are helping them to use their intellects to create those favorable circumstances which allow the orgasm to develop with no thought at all. (b) The extremely short foreplay period followed by quite intense orgasms is the usual situation in the higher primates; yet this is very different from most mammals where the long, teasing foreplay periods are the rule. In the mammalian animals below the primates, the delaying tactics so regularly employed by the females constitute an adaptive device which insures the integrity of the reproductive isolation of the species; the delay allows time for full species recognition preventing inadvertent cross-breeding.* In addition, the prolonged courtship is an adaptation insuring optimal reproductive success because it allows time for the rival mates to conduct their courtship battles with the breeding premium going to the strongest and most intelligent.

However, in the long-lived, higher social primates living in their hierarchically organized, permanent troops or close family groups, the delay mechanism is no longer necessary. The primate female may become extremely sexually aggressive, actively soliciting coitus, with copulations occurring rapidly and repetitively without danger to herself or to the species.

* This species-isolating mechanism is especially important for solitary, nocturnal animals or those living at the periphery of their geographical domain where they are more apt to run into animals of related species with whom infertile matings or even traumatic copulation might occur (49).

The human female does not experience the intense estrus edema of many primates; nonetheless, I submit that she *usually* requires a more prolonged foreplay period than the male for two reasons. First, the greater volume capacity of the venous plexi and the cyclic variations of responsivity require it *because* of the absence of a particular heat cycle. Secondly, a prolonged foreplay continues to exert a culturally salutary influence, reinforcing its retention. This is the deep awareness that it encourages men to assume the aggressive, masculine role and women, the passive, feminine role in love-making. The first point is the least important because women's responsivity is quite high, especially during the fourteen days directly preceding menstruation; it compares much more closely to the primates than to the lower mammalian females. If this reasoning is valid, we have an example of the reciprocal action of physical and cultural evolutionary processes. It also is evidence for the concept that direct sexual aggressiveness or passivity in humans is largely culturally determined.

14. Multiple Orgasms

An observation by Masters and Johnson which has received, surprisingly, not the least attention in the psychoanalytic or any psychiatric literature, I believe, is the normal and regular occurrence of multiple orgasms in women. The authors state (48, p. 792):

> If a female who is capable of having regular orgasms is properly stimulated within a short period after her first climax, she will *in most instances* be capable of having a second, third, fourth, and even a fifth and sixth orgasm before she is fully satiated. As contrasted with the male's usual inability to have more than one orgasm in a short period, many females, *especially when clitorally stimu-*

lated, can regularly have five or six full orgasms within a matter of minutes [italics added].

Multiple orgasms in women are well explained by the physiodynamics of the sexual cycle. To be stressed are the observations on three events during the resolution period: clitoral return to its resting position of pudendal overhang; detumescence of the lower third; and decoloration of the labia minora. These three events all occur simultaneously and with the same rapidity which characterizes the first-stage loss of the erection in the male. Since first-stage detumescence in men (see above) is produced primarily by the emptying of the penile bulb, I suggest that the immediate result of the orgasmic contractions in the female are: (a) emptying of the vestibular bulbs and commissure; (b) emptying of the circumvaginal plexi; and (c) relaxation of the ischiocavernosus muscles of the crura and the suspensory ligament from the rectus abdominus allowing clitoral return.

However, with full venous engorgement and edema, the plexi and emptied bulbar cavities refill immediately, and fluid from the tissues moves back into the vascular bed. With continued erotic stimulation, retraction of the clitoris again occurs; the muscles are soon stretched to the point of reflex contractions; and another orgasm occurs. (Some women prefer continuous stimulation, going from one orgasm to the next with practically no time lapse; others prefer to return to the plateau or excitement phase for restimulation to the next orgasm.)

Hence, the necessity and capacity for three to six or many more orgasms in a short time are explained, as well as why no orgasm (or a single weak one) leaves a woman who has been adequately aroused feeling uncomfortable, and why it takes so long for sexual tension to subside when no orgasm occurs. Not only must the engorged venous plexi return to normal, but the resorption of the tissue edema by the gradual process of osmosis must take place.

15. Labia Majora

For evolutionary biology, the disappearance of the labia majora in women who have never given birth is an observation of prime importance. The authors give no explanation for this phenomenon, but Masters (41) presented the possibility which had suggested itself to me from study of the primates: the response is homologous to the elevation of the testes and scrotum in the male during sexual arousal.

The labia majora move laterally and upward becoming flattened against the perineal floor. Being composed of loose fatty pigmented tissue (and nonvascular in women who have never borne children), they do not participate in the pelvic congestion and edema. In men, the testes are elevated against the perineum mostly by the cremasteric muscles in the spermatic cords. In women, the same action on the labia could be effected by the homologue of the cords, the round ligaments, which run from the uterus through the inguinal canals to end blindly in the tissues of the labia majora. These ligaments are curiously large and strong for a rudimentary, nonfunctional structure (see Fig. 3), and they are very rarely vestigial or absent. They are, interestingly, equally large in all the primates examined for them, *even though most have no labia majora at all* except during fetal life. In their proximal sections, the ligaments contain muscle fibers which could contract to elevate the labia; or the upward movement of the uterus during arousal could elevate the labia; or both actions could be involved. If so, it is understandable why the ligaments do not function in women who have had several successive pregnancies, where stretching from pregnancies would render them slack and where full vascularization and stretching of the labia have occurred.

The vascularization of the labia majora with pregnancies dramatically exemplifies the enormous extent of blood-vessel growth of which the pelvic tissues are capable and which the pregnancy hormones induce. During intense sexual arousal, in women who have successfully borne several children, the labia majora become so edematous and engorged that their resolution may require many hours. Obviously expulsion of blood from them does not form a part of the orgasmic response.

The expression Masters and Johnson use to describe the swollen labia, "hanging like folds of a heavy curtain," reminds one of the labia Schürzen *or aprons of certain tribal people mentioned by Ford and Beach (15) and by Devereux (12). In the light of the Masters and Johnson findings, one wonders if the permanently enlarged labia of these people could be due to very early and repeated pregnancies with frequent, full sexual arousal. Genetic factors and the intentional pulling on the labia for cosmetic purposes could also be involved.*

It is in relation to the production of multiple orgasms, I submit, that the true functioning of the labia majora may be appreciated. Heretofore, no important functional significance has been attached to these homologues of the scrotal sac other than the ill-defined function of their erotogenicity and their imputed action of being a "protective cushion" for the supposedly more delicate structures of the vestibule. I would postulate that the labia have no protective functioning at all. (The vestibular structures are not so delicate and the labia majora only add to the crowding and foster bacterial growth.) Their erotogenicity is not much more than that of the suprapubic skin. Rather, they act as reservoirs of congested vessels and edema, thereby aiding in the production of multiple orgasms. (Although the labia majora disappear in women who have not borne children, they begin to fill out again after prolonged stimulation and several orgasms; however, they never reach the point of extreme swelling seen in women having had multiple pregnancies.) The labia are not emptied during orgasms; venous return from them goes directly into the bulbar and pudendal plexi. *Continuous labial congestion and edema constitute a paramount factor in maintaining the sensation of intense perineal and pelvic congestion and of sexual tension.* Consequently, the more inexperienced women with undistended labia majora can feel more satisfied with one orgasm or two; for the woman who has borne many children, no matter how many "fully satisfying" orgasms she may have, she will not feel completely satiated until she is physically exhausted. One might say that in the maintenance of continuous sexual tension, the labia majora constitute the "largest plank" in the orgasmic platform.

16. Relationship of Multiple Orgasms to Clitoral Stimulation

Masters and Johnson have observed that many multiple orgasms are more apt to occur with autostimulatory techniques than with intravaginal coition. The reason is obvious, I think, in that few males can maintain an erection long enough for more than three to four orgasms in the woman. It must be recalled that all women must be stimulated continuously, especially during the plateau and orgasmic phases, or the level of sexual tension will drop almost instantaneously. Contrary to the male's, the female's muscles of orgasmic response will not continue to contract involuntarily;* hence an orgasm may be interrupted at any point.

---

* The difference has not been explained. It would be interesting to determine if the same difference exists in animals, and if there is an actual difference in the neural end organs of the muscles or in the muscle fibers themselves.

Counting two and a half minutes for a fully developed plateau phase in a woman with a high degree of vasocongestion and another two minutes for three successive orgasms, a man must maintain an erection for a minimum of four and a half minutes with active intravaginal thrusting; nor does this take into consideration that the time of the onset of the plateau phase is not evident to either partner, that penetration usually occurs during the excitement phase, and that many women prefer (or are obliged) to return to a lower level of tension before being restimulated to the next orgasm, thus prolonging the time the erection must be maintained to ten or fifteen minutes or more.

Therefore, it is understandable why multiple orgasms beyond three or four must usually be induced by continued clitoral stimulation. In sexual cycles produced by direct mons-area stimulation, a woman can control her own response level and "will experience *5 to 20 recurrent orgasmic experiences* with the sexual tension never allowed to drop below a plateau phase maintenance level until physical exhaustion terminates the session" (46, p. 256; italics added).

Mechanism for the Production of Multiple Orgasms—The Masters group has confirmed R. L. Dickinson's finding (13) that prolonged masturbation does not produce clitoral growth except in some instances of "measurable increases" in glans diameter in individuals using mechanical methods of stimulation (46, p. 255). Masters (41) gives the following explanation of this: "The average female with optimal arousal will usually be satisfied with 3–5 manually-induced orgasms; whereas mechanical stimulation, as with the electric vibrator, is less tiring and induces her to go on to long stimulative sessions of an hour or more during which *she may have 20 to 50 consecutive orgasms.* She will stop only when totally exhausted. Such sessions, occurring as often as 2–3 times a week, create a chronic passive congestion of the pelvis and work-hypertrophy of the clitoral shaft" (italics added).

In clinical practice, a number of married and single women using the electric vibrator to achieve up to fifty orgasms in a single session have come to my attention in the past few years. To have the comfort of a label, I had considered them to be cases of nymphomania without promiscuity. From the standpoint of our cultural norm, this may be an accurate enough phrase. From the standpoint of normal physiological functioning, these women exhibit a healthy, uninhibited sexuality—and *the number of orgasms attained, a measure of the human female's orgasmic potentiality.*

Moreover, Masters and Johnson found that *uterine contractions are regularly stronger in cycles produced by masturbation than in cycles produced by coition.* Assuming contractile strength is due primarily to the degree of congestion of the uterine walls, I suggest the more prolonged and effective stimulation gained by clitoral area friction must create a fuller pelvic congestion and stronger uterine contractions. Similarly, fuller pelvic congestion with clitoral stimulation accounts for the greater likelihood the external rectal sphincter contractions (see Chart I) will eventuate than with vaginally induced stimulation.*

It has been emphasized that, during coition, constant clitoral stimulation is maintained by friction of the prepuce against the glans via penile thrusting. Such light stimulation may seem inconsequential compared to the friction maintainable with digital masturbation. However, Masters and

* Masters (41) has unpublished preliminary findings on male homosexuals practicing anal intercourse. These men show marked hypertrophy of the hemorrhoidal plexi, which respond to arousal with vasodilation and *flow of transudate into the rectum.* The circumrectal musculature acts as the circumvaginal muscles, producing strong, multiple orgasms. Glans stimulation continues to be essential to erotogenic stimulation. The responsitivity of the pelvic plexi to sexual hormones in structuring vaginal cavities is amazing. No doubt the unusual cases in which the urethra is stretched until intercourse can take place in it (13) will show the same hypertrophy and sexual permeability of the urethral plexus.

Johnson use the expression "mons area stimulation" advisedly. During masturbation and during coital foreplay, practically no woman prefers to have the clitoris stimulated directly, or if so, only briefly. Direct clitoral contact, especially if any pressure is applied, is painful, decreasing sexual tension. In masturbation, digital application is usually made to the entire mons area with the finger being placed to the right or the left of the clitoral shaft depending on handedness.

I suggest that the reasons for the effectiveness of this manner of stimulation are: (a) there is such a small amount of erectile tissue in the shaft, any direct pressure would hinder whatever engorgement is possible; (b) the tiny glans is the most sensitive of all erotogenic zones (after the orgasm, it is quite painful to touch); hence direct friction could irritate rather than stimulate it; (c) pressure on the nonerect, retroflexed shaft could interfere with its upward retraction, which does not occur until the plateau phase, when continuous stimulation is most desired; and (d) most important, mons-area friction will have exactly the same effect on the prepuce-glans action as the penile thrusting motion: *the prepuce is rhythmically pulled back and forth over the glans.*

I would propose a further conclusion. Just as traction on the labia maintains the glans at a high level of stimulation during coition, so will mons-area stimulation place rhythmic traction on the swollen labia, stimulating the bulbs and the lower third in the reverse direction. Hence mons-area stimulation goes far beyond the clitoris itself, stimulating all the structures of primary response, just as penile friction during thrusting goes far beyond the lower third, stimulating all the structures of primary response.

Comments.—The common idea that clitorally induced orgasms are confined to the clitoris and are necessarily less satisfying *physically* than vaginally induced orgasms is manifestly erroneous. In addition, the popular idea that a woman should have one intense orgasm which should bring "full satisfaction," act as a strong sedative, and alleviate sexual tension for several days to come is simply fallacious. It should be stressed that the intensities of the multiple orgasms do not abate until fatigue of the responding muscles has set in. Each orgasm is followed promptly by refilling of the venous erectile chambers, distension creates engorgement and edema, which create more tissue tension, etc. The supply of blood and edema fluid to the pelvis is inexhaustible.

Consequently, the more orgasms a woman has, the stronger they become; the more orgasms she has, the more she *can* have. To all intents and purposes, *the human female is sexually insatiable in the presence of the highest degrees of sexual satiation.*

Some of the far-reaching implications of this understanding of women's paradoxical orgasmic potentiality will be presented in another volume; other implications, such as its influence and women's unconscious awareness of it on their personality structures and behavior, I have only begun to think about. At this time, I want to indicate two of the implications in line with the limited biological and cultural scope of this examination.

First, the nature of the sexual responsivity described is too close to that of certain higher primates to be ignored. I would suggest (and will take to be true) that the use of the Masters and Johnson techniques on these primates, with sexual anatomy so similar to the human female's, will reveal the same condition of *satiation-in-insatiation.* Having no cultural restrictions, these primate females will perform coitus from twenty to fifty times a day during the peak week of estrus, usually with several series of copulations in rapid succession. If necessary, they will flirt, solicit, present, and stimulate the male in order to obtain successive coitions. They will "consort" with one male for several days until he is exhausted, then take up with another. They will emerge from periods of heat totally exhausted, often with wounds from spent males who have repulsed them. I suggest that something akin to this behavior could be paralleled by the human female if her civilization allowed it.

(The nearly universal sentiment, still very prevalent in our Hebrew-Christian culture, that the female of the species does not, need not, or should not require orgasmic release (see Deutsch's opinion, p. 23) can now be said to be biologically unthinkable. The selective advantage for reproductive success of the orgasm in males is unquestionably accepted. The fact that the human female can be impregnated without an orgasm is hardly proof that such is biologically normal. That the female could have the same orgasmic anatomy (all of which is female to begin with) and not be expected to use it simply defies the very nature of the biological properties of evolutionary and morphogenetic processes. With the mammalian female carrying the bigger burden for the perpetuation of the species, in reproduction and care of the young, there is no logic in the idea that selection pressure, selecting for the reproductive advantage of the orgasmic capacity of the male, should find this same capacity disadvantageous and unrewarding for the female. And from all the foregoing, it is clear that the entire evolution of the sexual edema, the bulbs and circumvaginal plexi, the preputial-glandar mechanism, and the responding muscles in the primate line, culminating in the human female, is evidence of the high breeding premium which is awarded the female's erotogenic *and* orgasmic competency.

Our myth of the female's relative asexuality is a biological absurdity.)

Secondly, the similarities are remarkable between this satiation-in-insatiation state of the primate and human females and the behavior ascribed to women during the pre-patriarchal Mesolithic period—and well into the Neolithic Bronze Age—of history. Moreover, throughout historic time —and even today—it could well be that women have indulged in the so-called "orgastic parties," having relations with one man after another, for precisely the purpose of gratifying this capacity for numerous, successive orgasms with coition.

CHAPTER 4

Supplemental Data on Vaginal Insensitivity

From all the Masters and Johnson data just presented with their heavy emphasis on the functional unity and reciprocal stimulation of the lower third, labia minora, clitoris, and penis, it is the more difficult to understand why women are not able to attain an orgasm during vaginal coition with the greatest of ease. It has been demonstrated that transferral of erotogenic zone from the clitoris to the vagina cannot possibly take place during development; yet we are left with the problem of "clitoral fixation" unexplained.

The Masters and Johnson observations support the conclusion that the more sensitive and functional the clitoral glans is, the better it operates in producing the orgasm with intravaginal thrusting. These findings force us to the conclusion that *there is no such thing as psychopathological clitoral fixation; there are only varying degrees of vaginal insensitivity and coital frigidity.*

Freud was right, of course, in placing such emphasis on the fact that the girl has two erotogenic zones, the clitoris and vagina, and that the vagina does not normally become functional until the pubertal maturation and the first coition.

However, the clitoris and the lower third are inseparable structures; and Freud did not know that the lower and, possibly, the upper vagina are derived from the urogenital sinus. Indeed, it grows as an upward extension of the vestibule; and in many primates, the entire vagina does not canalize until the first estrus period. All these structures in males are anatomically female during the earliest stage of life. In males, the penis and bulb form by fusion of the bilateral corpora cavernosa, bulbs, and labia minora; the scrotum forms by fusion of the labia majora. Hence we may say that the external genitalia of the female are homologous to the entire penis split open along its undersurface and the split-open scrotal sac.

Psychoanalysis discerned long ago that people unconsciously (and often consciously) have always thought of the female genitalia as resembling, or being, a gash or a wound. However, the marvelous wisdom of children's conscious and adults' unconscious minds have been led astray here by the superficial appearances. The wound-like split-open, reddened parts are actually covered with a highly sensitive, mucous-membranelike epithelium which is, all things considered, extraordinarily tough and disease-resistant.

With maturation, the erotogenic zone of the lower third of the vagina does not supplant the clitoral zone; *it must be assimilated with the entire clitoral-labial complex into a single functional structure.* Many and diverse forces may interfere with this assimilation.

BIOLOGICAL FACTORS IN THE ETIOLOGY OF VAGINAL INSENSITIVITY

It will not be possible to outline the psychological factors operative in the development of coital frigidity in this already long study. Rather than slight these factors, so important to us, it seems best to conclude with a résumé of the more strictly physical factors interfering with vaginality and leave the psychological forces to another study. I believe that a comprehensive grasp of the physical factors impeding normal coital functioning is absolutely indispensable to the unfinished task of formulating an adequate understanding of the psychological inhibitions to the incorporation of the vagina into the body's total erotogenic resources. Moreover, since these findings and hypotheses call for rather drastic revisions of biological, psychological, and cultural concepts of female sexuality, it is paramount that all possible evidence be presented for evaluation.

The various genetic, constitutional, and acquired neuro-hormonal disorders affecting the development of vaginality are many, but are infrequently encountered in psychiatric practice. The present discussion, therefore, is limited to the problems surrounding our understanding of the development of normal vaginal erotism.

The most important biological barrier to vaginal assimilation beginning in childhood is the very nature of its development. The existence of infantile vaginality is another important question for psychoanalytic theory. I am not aware of any biological studies establishing beyond doubt the age at which a girl begins to experience vaginal sensations; nor can there be until the question of the actual *existence* of vaginal sensations in childhood and their importance in adulthood is established beyond doubt.

The question must now be put in different terms. We must establish the relative importance of the erotogenicity of the lining of the lower third of the vagina completely separated from the erotogenicity of the labial-preputial-glandar mechanism. Of course, this is almost impossible to determine from actual observations of coitus, since stimulation of the lower third necessarily activates the glandar-preputial mechanism. The Masters and Johnson studies, evolutionary biology, and other sources point to a number of factors which must be explained before any evaluation of eroto-genicity of the lower third and the nature of its development in humans can be made. In what follows I have listed a number of points, some of which have not been made be-fore, at least in this context. It will be seen that these data lend support to the thesis that the vaginal mucous mem-brane alone is relatively unimportant as an erotogenic zone.

Evidence from Evolutionary Biology

1. The evolutionary diversification of the labial-preputial-glandar mechanism in primates is of fantastic proportions. Both anatomical variations and hormonal responses of the labia, prepuce, and glans are involved. This is a good meas-ure of the value which selection pressure accords these structures in the attainment of reproductive success.

2. No evolutionary diversification of the lower third is evident except for devices (in only one species) which help retain the penis within the vagina, so that the glans probably does not touch the lower third during thrusting.

3. The variable presence and amounts of the vestibular bulbs and the perineal edema in species and within individ-uals of each species strongly suggest that the breeding pre-mium goes to the females with the most distensible bulbs, vaginal plexi, and the most edema. There is no indication that the lower third displays any kind of variability which would allow the breeding premium to go to the female with the greatest capacity for vaginal erotism. (The presence or ab-sence of the bulbs is guessed at according to their presence or absence in the males.)

4. In many primates, the vagina is a solid core of epithe-

lial cells throughout infancy and the juvenile period; the core center sloughs out, creating the vaginal space, just before the first period of heat. It is difficult to see how any tactile sensitivity can be ascribed to this solid core; nor is it known when or how neural connections and functioning are first achieved.

5. In all primates, cornification of the vagina during estrus, or heat, is intense; especially around the lower-third area, the layer of cornified cells seems almost too thick to permit much sensitive discrimination. (In humans, cornification is less marked.)

6. I am not aware of any reports describing vaginal exploration or masturbation in juvenile primates with or without the canalized vagina at birth. There are numerous reports mentioning clitoral-area exploration and masturbation throughout the juvenile period.

7. Ineffectual attempts at vaginal masturbation in isolated, caged primates have been reported, but only in such species as the chimpanzees in which the perineal swelling during estrus is huge, with the vaginal orifice opening prominently at its top. In the other species where the vaginal orifice remains deeply buried, it is so rarely discovered that there are no observations of attempts at vaginal stimulation. Clitoral masturbation is constantly observed in these isolated animals.

8. In many mammals, including many primates, the lower portion of the "vagina" is actually the urogenital sinus, a deep tubular structure which, with the clitoris in its anterior wall, has not exteriorized to form the long vestibule present in humans. At estrus, part of this tubular vestibule everts, bringing the clitoris into fuller view and forming the swollen labia. Hence the clitoris remains closely positioned within the urogenital sinus so that glans and shaft are more directly exposed to the thrusting movements of the penis during coitus. During coitus, the penile shaft is largely con-

tained within the urogenital sinus with only the glans reaching up into the vagina proper beyond the internal hymenal ring.

In many species, not only is the vagina proper occluded until puberty, but it reoccludes after each estrus or each pregnancy (or the hymen may grow back after each estrus or pregnancy). Only after many pregnancies will the labial folds remain permanently enlarged, so that a fairly large external vulvar groove is created. In brief, many mammalian females seem to be stimulated only on the clitoris and the still partially internalized urogenital sinus. Stimulation of the vagina proper is minimal or totally absent. There is no evidence that these females experience any less sexual tension than those with the permanently exteriorized vestibule and clitoris (except when compared to the higher primates where the additional factors of the sexual skin and highly effective preputial action must be taken into consideration).

Evidence from the Masters and Johnson Data

1. In the patients with artificial vaginas, the very rapid development of coital orgasms (within three months in one patient) suggests that the orgasms were attained by the labial-preputial-glandar mechanism alone—unless sensory nerve fibers into the new lower third regenerated far more rapidly than nerve fibers do elsewhere.

2. One of the significant differences between cycles in women and men is the fact that the male erection occurs almost instantaneously with arousal, whereas the timing of the clitoral erection (retraction) has become genetically separated from penile erection. The clitoris does not retract until an average of one and a half to two minutes before the orgasm. Therefore, the preputial-glandar stimulation exists for only those few minutes before the orgasm; and it must be

continued throughout the orgasm. No instance is reported in which clitoral erection took place during the excitement phase, as in men, and no instance of an orgasm occurring without clitoral erection has been observed.

3. This separation of the timing of the erections in males and females is an example of an evolutionary adaptation which probably required countless years to achieve. (Originally, the first mammals and first primates had sexual apparatuses very much alike in structure and functioning—many still do.) Since the timing separation is present in all women (and, I assume, in all primate females, since prolonged clitoral erections have not been reported), it must mean that some breeding advantage went to the ancestral primates in which this occurred. I would suggest that the essence of this reaction is the fact that glans stimulation via labial traction does not come into the erotogenic build-up until just before the orgasm, at the propitious moment, to give the final surge of vasotension necessary for the orgasm. If the orgasm were to occur earlier, there would be insufficient time for the build-up of the marked congestion and edema of the orgasmic platform so essential for intense and multiple orgasms. It does not seem credible that this kind of genetic variation in *glans* timing would have taken place unless glans stimulation was indispensable to the production of the kind of orgasms leading to the greatest mating and reproductive success.

4. A universal feature of the response cycle in women is the necessity for continuous stimulation. If stimulation is stopped even in the middle of the orgasm, the orgasm stops. This is true with clitoral-area and vaginally induced orgasms. Since a woman can gain a certain degree of vaginal stimulation with the slightest movement on her part against the erect or semierect penis, it seems logical to assume that such abrupt cessation of sexual tension would not be universal *if* the lower third were an erotogenic zone equal to the

clitoris. Cessation of the thrusting motion automatically stops the preputial-glandar action unless the woman is in the superior position and can continue the active motion herself —which may be why many women prefer this position.

5. In all instances of multiple orgasms with coition, Masters and Johnson report no case in which successive orgasms were produced by vaginal stimulation alone, i.e., the clitoris is always re-retracted and stimulated anew against the prepuce before each orgasm. If the vagina were a strong erotogenic zone, once an orgasmic level of vasotension were achieved, it seems logical to suppose that vaginal stimulation alone might carry through the successive orgasms. Since the thrusting motion inevitably brings the preputial-glans action into play, whether or not it is needed, vaginal stimulation alone would occur when the male completes his ejaculation and attempts to continue the woman's stimulation with digital manipulation. If the vagina were a strong erotogenic focus, women would definitely prefer such intravaginal digital stimulation with no clitoral stimulation. I believe that women never, or rarely, express this preference.

6. If vaginal erotism were effective, one would expect the combined stimulation of the lower third and glans during intravaginal coition to render such vaginally induced orgasms *more* readily attained, *more* intense, and *more* apt to eventuate in multiple orgasms than with clitoral-area stimulation alone. The reverse is usually true. Most women clearly prefer vaginally induced orgasms for good and sufficient emotional reasons, which are much the same reasons why men prefer coitus to masturbation—masturbation is a lonely affair. However, the data indicate that clitorally induced orgasms may be, and often are, as intense as vaginally induced ones and multiple orgasms are *more* likely to occur. Moreover, uterine and rectal contractions are more likely to occur with clitoral stimulation, indicating greater pelvic

vasocongestion. A highly erotic lower third should have the same vasotensive effect but does not. In other words, women will usually prefer vaginally induced orgasms, but not because the sheer physcal pleasure is greater, either in intensity or frequency of orgasmic release.

7. The duration of the excitement phase remains fairly constant for each woman, except under conditions of optimal arousal, generally varying with predictable variables. If the vagina were an intense erotogenic zone, one might expect Phase I to be regularly shortened by early penetration; the reverse is true in that Phase I is shortened by clitoral-area stimulation which brings on clitoral retraction sooner, thereby permitting more prolonged preputial-glandar action. Most women report more certain and intense orgasms if there is clitoral stimulation in Phase I. I have never heard of a woman reporting more certain and intense orgasms with only intravaginal digital stimulation during the foreplay. Yet this should occur if the lower third were an effective erotogenic zone.

8. In those patients with lax vaginal outlets caused by obstetrical damage, infrequent and weak orgasms during vaginal coition are usual, or none at all. Yet except in cases with very major degrees of outlet stretching and muscle damage, one would expect that the marked swelling of the lower third during the plateau phase would permit sufficient friction to effect vaginal stimulation, although not the preputial-glandar action. Hence there should be relatively little decrease in orgasmic competency, except with major degrees of vaginal gaping, if vaginal erotism were so effective. This is not so.

9. Similarly, in women who have not borne children and have a tight fourchette and high perineum, entry may be more difficult, but a close contact between the penile shaft and the lower third should be easier to achieve. Hence maximum stimulation of the lower third would be attained during

thrusting. If the lower third were a highly effective erotic zone, one would assume that vaginally induced orgasms would occur with the greatest of ease and frequency in women who have not borne children rather than in those who have. This is not so.

Evidence from Other Sources

1. Many women attempt "vaginal" masturbation; this seems almost always to be stimulation of the outlet area involving movement of the labia and the vestibule which would activate the preputial-glandar mechanism. Deep digital penetration of the lower third is unusual. I have never known a case of a woman, especially one who could achieve orgasms with coition, to resort to vaginal masturbation in the absence of coitus; they resort to clitoral-area stimulation. In addition, I have never known a woman who, once she has discovered that an orgasm can be attained by stimulation of the outlet area, continued in stimulating this area as the only and preferred form of autostimulation. If anything, they utilize what the Italians call (so I am told) "the three-finger method" which should apply effective stimulation to the entire vulvar and clitoral areas. (No doubt this technique is not an original Italian discovery.)

2. Accidental stimulation of the clitoral area often produces erotic sensations, even in children. Accidental stimulation of the lower third, as from the insertion and removal of tampons, douche tips, etc., does not produce similar erotic sensations, even if these procedures are performed during the height of the last half of the fourteen-day phase or during the excitement and plateau levels of sexual tension.

3. An incorrectly placed vaginal tampon touches the lower third. Even if the contact with the lining of the lower third is slight, it never creates erotic sensation; it produces irritation. If the contact is prolonged, it produces pain.

4. Women have been known to use almost every conceivable elongated object to substitute for the phallus in vaginal stimulation; yet none of these is particularly effective or has become popularly used. The most effective objects are those which are a close facsimile of the erect penis, primarily in diameter, not length—and even these are rarely used exclusively.

5. In practically all animals and with some humans (and probably in most early human cultures), the dorsal-ventral position for coitus is used. I suggest that, in humans, the female prefers this position as much as, if not more than, the male because the preputial-glandar mechanism works more efficiently. Being in the dependent position, the labial, preputial, and clitoral congestion and edema would occur more readily and be maintained well over a longer period.

6. Any woman can contract the responding muscles voluntarily (as can men), producing compression of the walls of the lower third. In the nonstimulated state, this should create considerable pressure friction on the normally collapsed walls and, one might think, arouse erotic feelings. Vaginal stimulation is rarely carried out in this manner; and I have never known a woman to produce orgasms with this form of stimulation. On the other hand, voluntary contractions of the adductor longus muscle has long been known to produce erotic arousal of the clitoris, since the tendons of that muscle can compress the labia majora against the clitoral shaft. It could well be that some women achieving orgasms by breast stimulation alone, or more probably, those who claim to achieve orgasms through erotic fantasies alone, could be adding to the level of sexual tension by the contraction of this muscle's tendons without being fully aware of it.

I would suggest that no one of these points is significant in itself. Taken together, however, and at the very least, they force us to the conclusion that much about the erotogenicity of the lower third of the vagina remains poorly understood. As matters now stand, these observations permit two tentative conclusions:

1. The labial-preputial-glandar action must be accorded a considerably higher potential of erotogenicity than the lower third of the vagina. It is doubtful that stimulation of the lower third of the vagina alone could produce anything but infrequent and weak orgasmic reactions at best.

2. It is extremely doubtful that vaginal sensations would occur in prepubertal girls. These observations indicate the strong likelihood that orgasms achieved by children are simply contractions of the responding muscles against the congested vestibular bulbs from clitoral-area stimulation, not involving vaginal erotism in any way or involving only very little congestion and edema from the still poorly developed circumvaginal plexus.

Subsequent research may give us alternative explanations for all these points which are not immediately discernible. Therefore, it seems wisest to postpone further hypotheses on the existence, nature, development, and adult functioning of vaginal erotism until such research materializes.

PHYSICAL FACTORS CAUSING COITAL FRIGIDITY BEGINNING IN ADULTHOOD

From the fundamental framework of the sheer physical aspects of the sexual cycle which has been given, it can be seen that coital frigidity will occur if there exists (a) inadequate erotogenic stimulation; (b) inadequate filling of the venous erectile chambers; (c) inadequate pelvic congestion and edema with their resultant tissue tension; and (d) inadequate response of the responding muscles. Many biological barriers may intervene at any point to produce varying degrees of frigidity. These biological barriers rarely, if ever, operate alone but induce psychological reactions reinforced by cultural pressures in endless vicious circles. Consequently, the differential diagnosis between vaginal insensitivity induced by physical factors or by psychological factors is often difficult to make. The following outline of the biological barriers stresses those problems where this diagnostic difficulty is most apt to arise in psychiatry.

Medical Disorders

Of the many diseases, disorders, and injuries which can affect the sexual structures, the following are most pertinent to psychiatry.

1. Obstetrical Damage

It has been emphasized that pregnancies enhance sexual capacity and pleasure by flooding the system with the sexual hormones, producing a sudden and enormous growth and vascularization of the pelvic structures as great as or greater, I believe, than the pubertal transformation. So important is the pregnancy effect, I would propose that the varicosities left by pregnancy are both adaptive and non-adaptive: during evolution, their value for the build-up and maintenance of sexual tension is so strong there could be nothing but increasing selective pressure for their presence.

However, evolutionary change often gets hoisted by its own petard, so to speak, and may or may not be able to extricate itself from an adaptational dilemma. These varicosities may be one such dilemma. Another, unfortunately, is the fact that the female sexual and procreative apparatus was evolved for mothers giving birth to small-headed babies. Man is much too recent an evolutionary innovation for the female pelvic adaptations necessary to deliver big-headed babies without trauma to the birth canal. (Of the 75,000,-000 years the primates have been working themselves up to us, men with heads big enough to produce consistent maternal damage have been around for only the past 500,000 years at most—and probably much less—perhaps .6 to .3 per cent of the total.) Obstetrical damage to the sexual structures is far more frequent than most psychiatrists realize, I believe. Without the best of modern obstetrical care, it occurs to a greater or lesser extent in close to 100 per cent of all women bearing their first full-term babies; and even with that care, it occurs to some degree in a very large number of them.

Severe traumas are uncommon in this country; moderate to mild degrees rarely abolish the capacity for orgasmic experience but usually lessen it. Furthermore, all obstetrical damage is most apt to occur during the first delivery. Thus, if a woman is unfortunate enough to suffer such damage before full sexual potency was attained, she may never realize the extent to which the obstetrical damage contributes to her frigidity.

Two most frequent forms of perineal tears are also most pertinent to this study:

a. *Tears of the Bulbar System*—Tears of the vestibular bulbs and their muscles are the main reason for episiotomies (which are not always done, done well, or become infected). The importance of the bulbar system to full orgasmic capacity is underscored by the fact that such tears are usually unilateral; gynecologists uniformly report that women with one nonfunctioning bulb regularly complain of diminished orgasmic reactions.

b. *Torn or Stretched Perineal Body*—The process of tears, scar formation, and stretching of all the muscles that make up the perineal body (see Fig. 4) is one of the most frequent causes of coital frigidity due to childbirth—a gaping vaginal orifice may make intercourse easy from the standpoint of ease of entry but can render the climax impossible to attain.

Masters describes an experiment with one volunteer which is particularly instructive on the nature of this problem as well as the dynamics of normal vaginal action (42). No history is available, of course, other than that this woman, who had previously successfully borne children, suffered coital frigidity as the result of obstetrical damage and had an exceptionally gaping vaginal outlet. The subject was obviously heterosexually oriented; so an experiment was designed to determine if she could possibly reach an orgasm if coitus were prolonged far beyond that which could possibly be achieved in personal life. The subject successfully carried coitus through twenty-seven times to the complete expenditure of nearly as many male partners over a six-and-a-half-hour period. No direct clitoral stimulation was allowed. Throughout this entire period, she remained in the excitement stage of arousal, achieving plateau stages of congestion on five occasions—but no orgasm occurred. At the end, pelvic congestion was severe and painful. The labia majora were three times their normal size; the labia minora and lower third of the vagina were greatly swollen and continued so; and it required one and a quarter hours for the breasts to return to normal. After the last coital effort, the patient was instructed to refrain from any autostimulation in order to determine how long it would require for this degree of pelvic congestion to subside. The pelvic structures were still uncomfortably swollen six hours later when the experiment (lasting twelve and a half hours) was declared terminated. The subject immediately sought relief in clitoral-area stimulation and achieved a violent orgasmic release of vasotension within two minutes.

This experiment is important to us on several scores:

(i) No matter how great the generalized pelvic congestion and edema, an orgasm will not eventuate unless there is that final surge of localized engorgement of the circumvaginal plexi and bulbs which causes the lower third to tighten around the penile shaft and permits the thrusting friction on the lower third and labia to activate the preputial-glandar action.

(ii) No matter how swollen the lower third, bulbs, and plexi become, they cannot tighten around the penile shaft if the vaginal outlet is abnormally widened.

(iii) Most significantly, it is obvious that the lower third was stimulated a great deal during this prolonged coital experience; it was greatly swollen. The weight of the penis on the posterior wall would create friction, if no place else. Yet this stimulation of the lower third was unable to produce the final high levels of sexual tension necessary for the orgasm. On the other hand, the gaping outlet, the lack of tightening of the lower third, and the elongated, loose, and widened labia minora would completely rule out the possibility of labial traction activating the preputial-glans mechanism. Hence, rhythmic stimulation of the glans could not occur. The rapidity and ease with which the clitorally induced orgasm subsequently occurred again point to the prime importance of this structure in the attainment of the orgasm.

Milder degrees of perineal lacerations are much more frequent than the type presented by this subject. They are, in a sense, more pernicious because they are easier to mistake for psychogenic frigidity. With the more moderate tears, the three all-important ingredients in the production of orgasmic levels of vasotension (gripping of the penile shaft; friction on the tightened lower third and upper labia; and labial-preputial-glandar action) may take place, but only if all conditions for full erotogenic arousal are optimal. With so little margin for all the innumerable physical and emotional variables which influence sexual performance, the orgasm would be achieved infrequently and, when achieved, would often be weak and disappointing.

2. *Constitutional and Endocrine Disorders*

Of the many disorders falling in these two categories, only two will be memtioned:

a. *Anatomical Variations*—A possible cause of coital frigidity, with its origin in genetic and endocrine factors and included here because they usually do not appear until after the pubertal transformation, are the anatomical variations of the labial-preputial anatomy. This subject has received no research interest—but should, in the light of the Masters and Johnson observations.

There seems to be so much variation in this anatomy that it is difficult to assign normal limits. For example, the prepuce may be doubled, tripled, or have accessory folds. It may be smooth, wrinkled, thick, thin, short, or elongated; it may be pigmented, follicle-studded, or adherent. Similarly, the labia minora show marked variations in size, may form two loops, or have accessory folds. They may be long, short, wrinkled, folded, or corrugated (13).

These common variations in the sexual anatomy may render the preputial-glandar action more difficult to attain with intravaginal coition, where only a taut connection between the upper labia around the vaginal orifice and the prepuce can create the necessary traction. Obviously, the adherent prepuce practically precludes the possibility of coital orgasms. The extent to which the other variations may interfere is unknown and requires the necessary research.

b. *Juvenile Pelvic Condition*—Many adolescents mature quite late and may retain a partially juvenile pelvic condition until after their first pregnancy. They may show scant menses, small breasts, boyish body contour, and coital frigidity. It must be kept in mind that specific levels of specific hormones must be present to permit the development of the congestion and edema which create the strong circumvaginal distension necessary for vaginally induced orgasms. Such hormonal levels are slow in developing in these young women (and may continue at low levels throughout life if they remain childless). The juvenile pelvic condition prevents full vasotension, so that the labial-preputial-glandar action is not effective. Most of the time, only a simple bulbar orgasm produced by digital stimulation is possible.

Inadequate Erotogenic Stimulation

Assuming an average good degree of pelvic vascularization in both the women who have and have not successfully borne children with no obstetrical damage or unusual anatomical variation, adequate physical stimulation is still necessary for coital orgasms to occur. Inadequate erotogenic stimulation is unquestionably the most frequent cause of vaginal frigidity. So much has been written on the subject, only some additional points made by Masters and Johnson relating to the central themes of this paper will be elaborated.

1. Continuous Stimulation

The fact that every woman's level of sexual tension falls almost instantaneously if stimulation is stopped accounts for many cases of frigidity, since most men over thirty (and many under) cannot consistently control their ejaculations long enough to permit the woman to reach full pelvic congestion. The one thing that prevents frigidity from this cause being more frequent is the young man's capacity to have repetitive ejaculations without full loss of the erection. Frequent coital frigidity in women whose husbands cannot have multiple orgasms, have them infrequently, or cannot hold their erections for at least four to five minutes is to be expected.

2. Slower Arousal Time in Women

A clinical impression is that a woman's inability to reduce the period of foreplay with increasing sexual experience is a frequent source of marital discord, if not of coital frigidity. If a man is quickly aroused and unaccustomed, or afraid, to use delaying techniques, coital frigidity would occur frequently or regularly.

3. *Luteal-Phase Sexuality*

An inability to achieve multiple orgasms, a reduced intensity of orgasmic sensations, and the capacity for only manually induced orgasms at all times other than the last fourteen days of the menstrual cycle may be considered normal. However, almost total frigidity (arousal only to an early excitement stage) or the consistent inability to achieve an orgasm with good levels of congestion in the plateau stage is rare enough in the ovulatory phase of the menstrual cycle to be considered evidence of either an abnormal hormonal condition or of psychological inhibitions of clinical significance.

4. *Attempting Clitoral Stimulation during Coitus*

Masters and Johnson stress that a very prevalent notion exists that the man must somehow keep the clitoral shaft directly stimulated during coitus. The physiodynamics of the sexual act indicate that such action is neither really possible nor helpful. In his effort to "ride high" during coition, a man is often unable to maintain intravaginal positioning unless there is an abnormally wide vaginal outlet; otherwise the main result is often the production of vaginal and rectal discomfort with the tip of the penis directed against the rectum.

5. *Special Problems Created by the Pregnancy Effect and Sexual Experience*

It has been noted that the orgasmic intensity is normally higher in the young, vigorous male than in the young woman who has not yet borne offspring. This difference levels off after about the age of thirty in men and after about the second or third child in women, or after considerable sexual experience. With age, experience, and successful childbirth, a woman's capacity for intense and multiple orgasms would surpass that of the man. I suggest that the oft-noted observation that modern women so often achieve the capacity for regular and multiple orgasms at about the time their husbands' performance is diminishing is due much more to the pregnancy effect and sexual experience than to any recovery from neurotic fears or inhibitions. The pregnancy effect has become increasingly delayed in many women today because of their more prolonged adolescence, later marriage age, and the use of contraceptives.* Fewer women reach their full sexual capabilities until after the age of thirty or so because they do not have their second or third child until that age.

Also, I urge the re-examination of the vague and controversial concepts of nymphomania and promiscuity without frigidity. Until now, it has not been realized that regular multiple orgasms, with either clitoral or vaginal stimulation, to the point of physical exhaustion could be the biological norm for women's sexual performance. Without undue inhibitions and with prolonged experience even the woman who has not yet borne offspring can approximate the high levels of vasocongestion reached by the already reproductive female. It could well be that the "oversexed" woman is actually exhibiting a normal sexuality—although because of it, her integration into her society may leave much to be desired.

6. Special Problems Created by Women's Satiation-in-Insatiation

No doubt the most far-reaching hypothesis extrapolated from these biological data is the existence of the universal and physically normal condition of women's inability ever

---

* In very recent years, with the population increases, coeducation, lack of college facilities, poor education motivations, and the increased sexual freedom allowed adolescents at earlier ages, a trend in the reverse direction of short adolescence and early marriage is also in full swing. The flux of our society is too marked to permit any generalization to apply for long. I believe we may expect to see both these trends continue for some time.

to reach complete sexual satiation in the presence of the most intense, repetitive orgasmic experiences, no matter how produced. Theoretically, a woman could go on having orgasms indefinitely if physical exhaustion did not intervene.

It is to be understood that repetitive orgasms leading to the satiation-in-insatiation state will be most apt to occur during the last fourteen days of the menstrual cycle in experienced women who have already borne children. It is one of the most important ways in which the sexuality of the primate and human female differs from the primate and human male at the physical level; and this difference exists only because of the female's capacity to produce the fulminating pelvic congestion and edema. This capacity is mediated by specific hormonal combinations with high fluid-imbibing action, which are found only in certain primates and, probably, a very few other mammalian species.

I must stress that this condition does not mean a woman is always consciously unsatisfied. There is a great difference between satisfaction and satiation. A woman may be emotionally satisfied to the full in the absence of *any* orgasmic expression (although such a state would rarely persist through years of frequent arousal and coitus without some kind of physical or emotional reaction formation). Satiation-in-insatiation is well illustrated by Masters' statement, "A woman *will usually* be satisfied with 3–5 orgasms . . ." (41). I believe it would rarely be said, "A man will usually be satisfied with three to five ejaculations." The man *is* satisfied. The woman *usually wills* herself to be satisfied because she is simply unaware of the extent of her orgasmic capacity. However, I predict that this hypothesis will come as no great shock to many women who consciously realize, or intuitively sense, their lack of satiation.

On the basis of these observations, it seems that the vast majority of cases of coital frigidity are due simply to the absence of frequent, prolonged coitus. This statement is supported by data which Masters and Johnson are now accumulating (41). Following this logical conclusion of their previous research, they began treating a series of couples with severe, chronic frigidity or impotence. All had received prior medical and, often, psychiatric treatment to no avail. For the women, none of whom had ever experienced orgasms after five or more years of marriage, treatment consisted of careful training of the husband to use the proper techniques essential to all women and the specific ones required by his wife. In many cases this in itself was sufficient. In the others, daily sessions were instigated of marital coitus followed by prolonged use of the artificial phallus (three to four hours or more). Thus far, with about fifty women treated, every woman but one responded within three weeks at most and usually within a few days. They began at once to experience intense, multiple orgasms; and once this capacity was achieved after the exposure to daily prolonged coitus, they were able to respond with increasing ease and rapidity so that the protracted stimulation was no longer necessary. It is too early for thorough follow-ups, but initial impressions are most favorable.

Should these preliminary findings hold, an almost total biological behavioral syndrome of coital frigidity will be demonstrated. The inordinate sexual, orgasmic capacity of the human female will fall in line with that of the other higher primates—and the magnitude of the psychological and social problems facing modern mankind is difficult to contemplate.

HISTORICAL PERSPECTIVE AND CULTURAL DILEMMA

The nature of female sexuality as here presented makes it clear that, just as the vagina did not evolve for the delivery of big-headed babies, so women's inordinate orgasmic capacity did not evolve for monogamous, sedentary cultures. It is unreasonable to expect that this inordinate sexual capacity could be, even in part, given expression within the confines of our culture; and it is particularly unreasonable to expect the delayed blooming of the sexuality of many women after the age of thirty or so to find adequate avenues of satisfaction. Less than one hundred years ago, and in many places today, women regularly had their third or fourth child by the time they were eighteen or nineteen, and the life span was no more than thirty-five to forty years. It could well be that the natural synchronization of the peak periods for sexual expression in men and women has been destroyed only in recent years.

These findings give ample proof of the conclusion that neither men nor women, but especially not women, are biologically built for the single spouse, monogamous marital structure or for the prolonged adolescence which our society can now bestow upon both of them. Generally, men have never accepted strict monogamy except in principle. Women have been forced to accept it; but not, I submit, for the reasons usually given.

The human mating system with its permanent family and kinship ties was absolutely essential to man's becoming—and remaining—man. In every culture studied, the crucial transition from the nomadic, hunting, and food-gathering economy to a settled, agricultural existence was the beginning of family life, modern civilization, and civilized man. In the preagricultural societies, life was precarious, population growth slow, and infanticide often essential to group survival. With the domestication of animals and the agricultural revolution, for the first time in all time, the survival of a species lay in the extended family with its private property, kinship lineages, inheritance laws, social ordinances, and, most significantly, many surviving children. Only in that carefully delineated and rigidly maintained large family complex could the individual find sufficient security to allow his uniquely human potentialities to be developed through the long years of increasingly helpless childhood—and could populations explode into the the first little villages and towns.

Many factors have been advanced to explain the rise of the patriarchal, usually polygynous, system and its concomitant ruthless subjugation of female sexuality (which necessarily subjugated her entire emotional and intellectual life). However, if the conclusions reached here are true, it is conceivable that the *forceful* suppression of women's inordinate sexual demands was a prerequisite to the dawn of every modern civilization and almost every living culture. Primitive woman's sexual drive was too strong, too susceptible to the fluctuating extremes of an impelling, aggressive erotism to withstand the disciplined requirements of a settled family life—where many living children were necessary to a family's well-being and where paternity had become as important as maternity in maintaining family and property cohesion. For about half the time, women's erotic needs would be insatiably pursued; paternity could never be certain; and with lactation erotism, constant infant care would be out of the question.

There are many indications from the prehistory studies in the Near East that it took perhaps 5,000 years or longer for the subjugation of women to take place. All relevant data from the 12000-to-8000 B.C. period indicate that precivilized woman enjoyed full sexual freedom and was often totally incapable of controlling her sexual drive.* There-

* "Today it is unfashionable to talk about former more matriarchal orders of society. Nevertheless, there is evidence from many parts of the world that the role of women has weakened since earlier times in several sections of social structure." The evidence given here lends further support to this statement by J. Hawkes and L. Woolley (22). However, I must make it clear that the biological data presented support only the

fore, I propose that one of the reasons for the long delay between the earliest development of agriculture (c. 12,000 B.C.) and the rise of urban life and the beginning of recorded knowledge (c. 8000–5000 B.C.) was the ungovernable cyclic sexual drive of women. Not until these drives were gradually brought under control by rigidly enforced social codes could family life become the stabilizing and creative crucible from which modern civilized man could emerge.

Although then (and now) couched in superstitious, religious, and rationalized terms, behind the subjugation of women's sexuality lay the inexorable economics of cultural evolution which finally forced men to impose it and women to endure it. If that suppression has been, at times, unduly oppressive or cruel, I suggest the reason has been neither man's sadistic, selfish infliction of servitude upon helpless women nor women's weakness or inborn masochism. The strength of the drive determines the force required to suppress it.

The hypothesis that women possess *a biologically determined,* inordinately high cyclic sexual drive is too significant to be accepted without confirmation from every field of sci-

---

thesis on the intense, insatiable erotism in women. Such erotism could be contained within one or possibly several types of social structures which would have prevailed through most of the Pleistocene period. I hope to elaborate on this complicated subject in a later paper.

I am indebted to Prof. Joseph Mazzeo of Columbia University for calling my attention to the fact that the first study on the existence of a pre-Neolithic matriarchal society was published in 1861: Bachofen's *Das Mutterrecht* (2). Indeed, Bachofen's work remains an unsurpassed, scholarly analysis of the mythologies of the Near East, hypothesizing both a matriarchal society and the inordinate erotism of women. His entire thesis was summarily rejected by twentieth-century anthropologists for lack of objective evidence (and cultural bias). On several scores, the ancient myths have proved more accurate than the modern scientists' theories. I suspect this will be another instance in which the myths prove faithful reflections of former days.

ence touching the subject. Assuming this analysis of the nature of women's sexuality is valid, we must ask ourselves if the basic intensity of women's sexual drive has abated appreciably as the result of the past 7,000 years of suppression (which has been, of course, only a partial suppression for most of that time). Just within the very recent past, a decided lifting of the ancient social injunctions against the free expression of female sexuality has occurred. This unprecedented development is born of the scientific revolution, the product both of efficient contraceptives and the new social equality and emotional honesty sweeping across the world (an equality and honesty which owe more to the genius of Sigmund Freud than to any other single individual). It is hard to predict what will happen should this trend continue —except that one thing is certain: if women's sexual drive has not abated and they prove incapable of controlling it, thereby jeopardizing family life and child care, a return to the rigid, enforced suppression will be inevitable and mandatory. Otherwise the biological family will disappear and what other patterns of infant care and adult relationships could adequately substitute cannot now be imagined.

Should the hypothesis be true that one of the requisite cornerstones upon which all modern civilizations were founded was *coercive* suppression of women's inordinate sexuality, one looks back over the long history of women and their relationships to men, children, and society since the Neolithic revolution with a deeper, almost awesome sense of the ironic tragedy in the triumph of the human condition.

S U M M A R Y

Recent embryological research has demonstrated conclusively that the concept of the initial anatomical bisexuality or equipotentiality of the embryo is erroneous. All mammalian embryos, male and female, are anatomically female during the early stages of fetal life. In humans, the differentiation of the male from the female form by the action of fetal androgen begins about the sixth week of embryonic life and is completed by the end of the third month. Female structures develop autonomously without the necessity of hormonal differentiation. If the fetal gonads are removed from a genetic female before the first six weeks, she will develop into a normal female, even undergoing normal pubertal changes if, in the absence of ovaries, supplemental outside hormones are supplied. If the fetal gonads are similarly removed from a genetic male, he will develop into a female, also undergoing normal female pubertal changes if additional outside hormones are supplied. The probable relationship of the autonomous female anatomy to the evolution of the bringing forth of live young has been described in this study.

From this surprising discovery of modern embryology

and other biological data, the hypothesis is suggested that the female's relative lack of differentiating hormones during embryonic life renders her more sensitive to hormonal conditioning in later life, especially to androgens, since some embryonic and strong maternal estrogenic activity is present during embryonic life. This ready androgen responsivity provides the physiological means whereby androgen-sensitive structures could evolve to enhance the female's sexual capacity. In the primates, the marked development of the clitoral system, certain secondary sexual characteristics, including skin erotism, and the extreme degree of perineal sexual edema (achieved in part by progesterone with its strong androgenic properties) are combined in various species to produce an intense aggressive sexual drive and an inordinate, insatiable capacity for copulations during periods of heat. The breeding advantage would thus go to the females with the most insatiable sexual capacity. The infrahuman female's insatiable sexual capacity could evolve only if it did not interfere with maternal care. Maternal care is insured by the existence of the extreme sexual drive only during periods of sexual heat and its absence during the prolonged post-pregnancy period, permitting the mother to devote her full attention to her offspring.

The validity of these considerations and their relevance to the human female are strongly supported by the demonstration of comparable sexual physiology and behavior in women. This has been accomplished by the research of Masters and Johnson, and a summary of their findings of the actual nature of the sexual response cycle in women has been presented here. Their most important observations are:

a. There is no such thing as a vaginal orgasm distinct from a clitoral orgasm. The nature of the orgasm is the same, regardless of the erotogenic zone stimulated to produce it. The orgasm consists of the rhythmic contractions of the ex-

travaginal musculature against the greatly distended circumvaginal venous plexi and vestibular bulbs surrounding
the lower third of the vagina.

b. The nature of the labial-preputial-glandar mechanism
which maintains continuous stimulation of the retracted clitoris during intravaginal coition has been described. By this
action, clitoris, labia minora, and lower third of the vagina
function as a single, smoothly integrated unit when traction
is placed on the labia by the male organ during coitus. Stimulation of the clitoris is achieved by the rhythmical pulling
on the edematous prepuce. Similar activation of the clitoris
is achieved by preputial friction during direct clitoral-area
stimulation.

c. With full sexual arousal, women are normally capable
of many orgasms. As many as six or more can be achieved
with intravaginal coition. During clitoral-area stimulation,
when a woman can control her sexual tension and maintain
prolonged stimulation, she may attain up to fifty or more
orgasms in an hour's time.

From these observations and other biological data, especially from primatology, I have advanced four hypotheses:

1. The erotogenic potential of the clitoral glans is probably greater than that of the lower third of the vagina. Additional evidence will be presented in the forthcoming volume
showing the importance of the labial-preputial-glandar action in the primates. The evolution of primate sexuality has
occurred primarily through selective adaptations of the
perineal edema and the clitoral complex, not the vagina.

2. Under optimal arousal conditions, women's orgasmic
potential may be similar to that of the primates described. In
both, orgasms are best achieved only with the high degree of
pelvic vasocongestion and edema associated with the defined
and limited period of heat in the primates and the last
fourteen days of the menstrual cycle in women or with prolonged, effective stimulation. Under these conditions, each

orgasm tends to increase pelvic vasocongestion; thus the more orgasms achieved, the more can be achieved. Orgasmic experiences may continue until physical exhaustion intervenes.

3. In these primates and in women, an inordinate cyclic sexual capacity has thus evolved leading to the paradoxical state of sexual insatiation in the presence of the utmost sexual satiation. The value of this state for evolution is clear: with the breeding premium going to the primate females with the greatest pelvic edema, the most effective clitoral erotism, and the most aggressive sexual behavior, the satiation-in-insatiation state may have been an important factor in the adaptive radiation of the primates leading to man— and a major barrier to the evolution of modern man.

4. The rise of modern civilization, while resulting from many causes, was contingent on the suppression of the inordinate cyclic sexual drive of women because (a) the tremendously increased supply of hormones of the early human females associated with the hypersexual drive and the prolonged pregnancies was an important force in the escape from the strict heat-cycle sexuality and the much more important escape from post-pregnancy diminished sexual desires. Women's uncurtailed continuous hypersexuality would drastically interfere with maternal responsibilities; and (b) with the rise of the settled agriculture economies, man's territorialism became expressed in property rights and kinship laws. Large families of known parentage were mandatory and could not evolve until the inordinate sexual demands of women were curbed.

Finally, the data on the embryonic female primacy and the Masters and Johnson research on the sexual cycle in women will require amendations of psychoanalytic theory. These will be less than one might think at first sight. Other than concepts based on innate bisexuality, the rigid dichotomy between masculine and feminine sexual behavior, and derivative concepts of the clitoral-vaginal transfer theory, psychoanalytic theory will remain what it has been. Much of the theory concerning the "masculine" components of female sexuality will also remain but will be based on a different biological conception. Certainly, much of present and past sexual symbolism will take on richer meanings.

It is my strong conviction that these fundamental biological findings will, in fact, strengthen psychoanalytic theory and practice in the area of female sexuality. Without the erroneous biological premises, the basic sexual constitution and its many manifestations will be seen as highly moldable by hormonal influences, which in turn are so very susceptible to all those uniquely human emotional, intellectual, imaginative, and cultural forces upon which psychoanalysis has cast so much light. The power of the psychic processes will stand the stronger. Therefore it may be safely predicted that these new biological findings will not "blow away" Freud's "artificial structure of hypotheses" but will transpose it to a less artificial and more effective level.

In any event, and regardless of the validity of my own conclusions, it is my hope that this presentation of recent major contributions from biology and gynecology bearing on female sexual differentiation and adult functioning will aid in the integration of psychological and biological knowledge, and will provide a firm biological foundation upon which all future theories of female psychosexuality must rest.

A PRIMER ON
SEXUAL ANATOMY

MEN

The penis is divided into three parts. Each part, in its own elastic sheath, is a long cylinder of erectile tissue with blood vessels and blood-filled spaces. Almost everyone thinks of the penis as simply the pendulous shaft hanging free in front of the scrotum, but this is only one half of it. The other half, containing the powerhouse for the orgasm and ejaculation, is hidden from view (I call it the cryptic portion). Lying at a right angle to the flaccid shaft, it is firmly embedded in the space between the testicles below and the prostate at the base of the bladder above (Fig. I). When erect the entire penis forms a straight line at right angles to the body.

In popular descriptions of the penis, the three parts are sometimes called "hollow bodies," a gross misnomer because the penis is never hollow. Actually the official Latin names of these parts and their muscles are rather awkward and confusing, although, of course, impeccably correct scientifically. Adequate synonyms in English are hard to come by; so a few medical terms will have to be endured.

There are two upper cylinders, called the *corpora cavernosa* (Fig. II), which literally means "bodies full of caverns," and the name is more or less appropriate depending

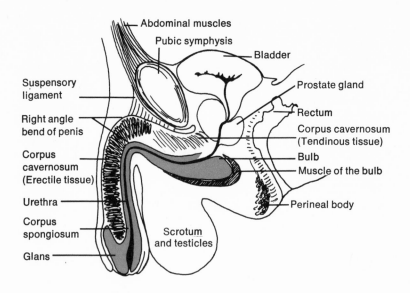

Figure I. Lateral view of the entire penis.

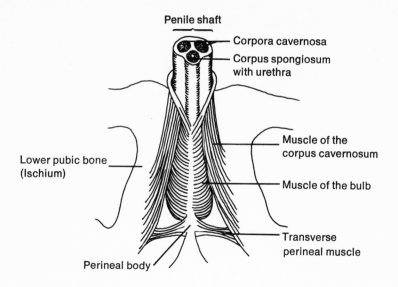

Figure II. **Muscles surrounding erectile columns of the penis.**

on one's notion of caverns—these being about the size of the head of a pin. Those who have studied the arrangement of these tiny chambers, which can render the penis as hard as a rock in an instant and deflate it with equal rapidity, marvel at the astounding hydraulic engineering. Indeed, a glance at the design of the caverns (Fig. III) makes it evident that no human engineer could have invented these.

The two upper cylinders of cavernous tissue lie side by side and are similar in structure. (Fig. II shows them from the underside and in cross-section.) The corpora cavernosa are solely responsible for the increased size, especially the greater width, and rigidity of the erect penis. In fact, when distended this double-barreled ramrod is so hard that its two pointed ends could damage the vagina or the penis itself were it not for the soft cushioning of the glans (Figs. I and IV). At the base of the pendulous shaft of the penis, the two columns diverge from each other and might now be called the legs of the penis; however, since it is comical to describe the penis as having legs, the official word in Latin for legs (*crura*; singular *crus*) would seem to be preferable. As the crura pass backward, they change into tough tendinous fibers which are securely attached to the inner surface of the lower pelvic bones (on which one sits). (Fig. I shows the tendinous change; Figs. II, IV, and V show the bony attachment.) Thus the corpora cavernosa of the penis have two functions: they anchor the shaft of the penis to its moorings and they provide the organ with most of its rigidity and increased size during erection, thereby rendering it capable of vaginal penetration.

The lower, underside cylinder of the penis (Figs. I, II, and IV) is quite different from the corpora cavernosa. It resembles a single-barreled shotgun with the bore being the *urethra,* the tube carrying urine and semen. The soft-walled urethra is prevented from collapsing during erection, thereby blocking the ejaculation, by remarkable little struts (Fig. III); and when the erection ends, although the walls of the

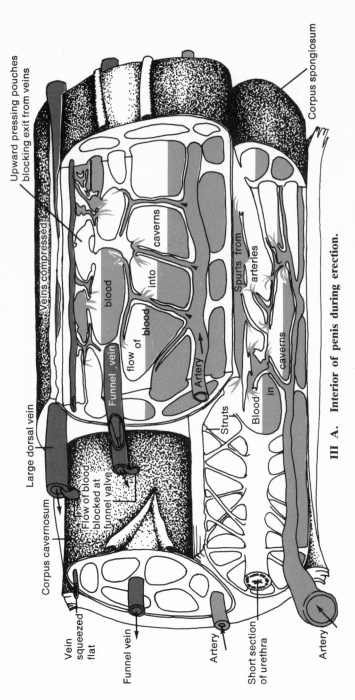

Figure III. Microscopic anatomy of erectile tissues. Redrawn from *Human Sex Anatomy*, 2nd ed., by Robert Latou Dickinson. Copyright 1949, Baltimore: The Williams & Wilkins Company.

III A. Interior of penis during erection.

Upward pressing pouches blocking exit from veins

Corpus spongiosum

Large dorsal vein

Veins compressed

Spurts from arteries

Funnel vein

flow of blood into caverns

Artery

Corpus cavernosum

Struts

Blood in caverns

Vein squeezed flat

Flow of blood blocked at funnel valve

Funnel vein

Artery

Short section of urethra

Artery

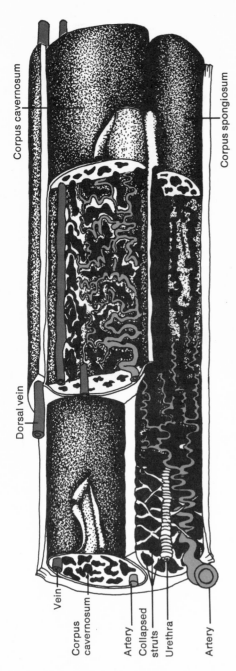

Corpus cavernosum

Corpus spongiosum

Dorsal vein

Vein

Corpus cavernosum

Artery

Collapsed struts

Urethra

Artery

III B. Interior of flaccid penis.

nozzle

III C. Diagram of a funnel vein.

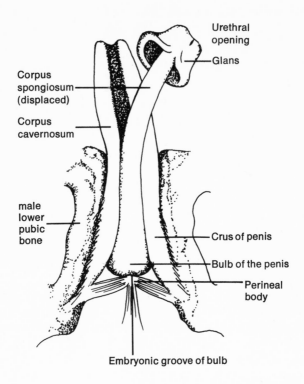

Urethral opening

Glans

Corpus spongiosum (displaced)

Corpus cavernosum

male lower pubic bone

Crus of penis

Bulb of the penis

Perineal body

Embryonic groove of bulb

Figure IV. **The structure of the erect penis viewed from below.**

urethra collapse like an accordion its inner tube remains functional.

This urethra-bearing cylinder is called the *corpus spongiosum* because it remains relatively soft (spongy) during the erection. The corpus spongiosum expands at its tip to form the glans and again at its base beneath the prostate to form the *bulb of the penis*. The glans enlarges to almost twice its usual size during the erection; but it remains the soft, protective cushion for the rigid corpora cavernosa. The bulb, on the other hand, has a structure similar to that of the corpora cavernosa, and although it is a part of the soft corpus spongiosum, it becomes quite rigid and distended during an erection.

There is a small groove encircling the end of the bulb (Fig. V) which is the only clue betraying the fact that once there were two bulbs in every male (in the early embryonic life of the male, the two bulbs fuse to produce the single bulb of the penis).

Because the two crura have changed into so much fibrous anchoring tissue, the bulb of the penis provides the largest volume of the cryptic erectile tissue, almost filling the space between the two pelvic bones (Figs. IV and V). When distended, the bulb lengthens and markedly increases in diameter, and presses down on the testicles.

The most important point to note is that the pendulous shaft of the penis is made up entirely of the three erectile bodies. There are no muscle fibers nor any other mechanism in this exposed part to produce an ejaculation. In the cryptic portion, however, each cylinder becomes enclosed in its muscular coat (Figs. I and II). These muscles, with some assistance from practically all other muscles in the area, are responsible for the final erection and the ejaculation. These muscles contract in a coordinated, downward-moving rhythm which compresses the erectile bodies, which, in turn, compresses the sperm tube, thereby forcing the semen for-

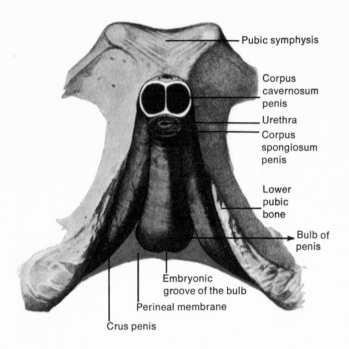

Figure V. The root of the penis. From *Cunningham's Textbook of Anatomy*, edited by G. J. Romanes and published by Oxford University Press as an Oxford Medical Publication.

ward with considerable force.* In other words, the outside pressure exerted by the muscular coats on the erectile tissue both forces the blood out of the distended cavernous spaces and compresses the urethra; the successive, wavelike compressions of the urethra force the ejaculation.

One other structure assisting in the erection deserves an honorable mention. This is the *suspensory ligament,* a thin band of fibrous tissue running from the upper margin of the penis at the bend of the pubic bone and into the fibrous coverings of the lower abdominal muscles (Fig. I). Although I know of no study verifying this, it is probably the suspensory ligament that is partially responsible for the voluptuous sensation experienced when the skin of the lower abdomen is stroked. Since the thigh muscle coverings are connected with those of the lower abdominal muscle coverings, the same sensation is experienced when the inner thighs are stroked.

There are special sensory nerve endings scattered throughout the muscle coats of the three cavernous bodies of the penis which respond only to stretching. Thus, when the distended bulb and corpora cavernosa have stretched their muscles beyond a certain point, the stimulated nerve endings signal the brain to set off the muscle contractions. (All the neuro-muscular pathways with their cerebral connections producing the precise muscular contractions of the orgasm are still not known to us.)

WOMEN

The penile and clitoral systems are exact homologues of each other. This means that each part in the one finds its

* The semen gets a weak initial push from the contraction of muscle fibers lying in a special mass of storage tubules near the testicles and in the ducts of the prostate gland. These structures play such a minor role in the physiology of the orgasm and ejaculation that they are not shown here or dealt with in the text.

counterpart in the other. The counterpart may be structurally the same in both, modified more or less to perform a different function (or to perform the same function in a different way), or if no functioning is required or possible, atrophied to a vestigial state. It is not necessary to describe the parts of the clitoral system that correspond so well to those of the male just presented. Figure VI shows the clitoral system and illustrates quite well the similarities to the penile system. The following discussion elaborates on the significant differences with particular emphasis on the nature of the orgasm in women during intercourse.

First, the corpora cavernosa in women function exactly as those in men except that they do not contain as many of those intake and output valves that have been described. Because the muscles of these bodies are prime movers in producing the erection, this means that women will initially have repeated erections and relaxations of the clitoris more easily than men. In addition, although the pendulous portion of the clitoris is greatly reduced in size compared to that of the penis, the crura remain as large as they would be if they were securing a full-sized shaft of the penis (Fig. VI). This gives the clitoral crura the incongruous appearance of a battleship's anchor tied to a rowboat.

Second, the size of the outlet of the bony pelvis in females is much wider than in males. Figure VII attempts to demonstrate this difference by superimposing one pelvis over the other using illustrations of approximately the same scale. Women's pelvic bones flare out much more widely than do men's; the crura of the corpora cavernosa must be correspondingly wider apart. With few exceptions, the true pelvic outlet of the smallest normal woman is larger than that of the largest man. (Although the joint of the pubic symphysis gives a little during pregnancy, in essence a woman's outlet and the vaginal wall must be wide enough to permit passage of the baby's head.)

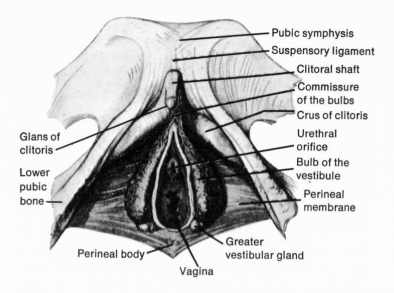

Figure VI.   Dissection of female perineum, showing the clitoris, the bulbs of the vestibule, and the greater vestibular glands. From *Cunningham's Textbook of Anatomy*, edited by G. J. Romanes and published by Oxford University Press as an Oxford Medical Publication.

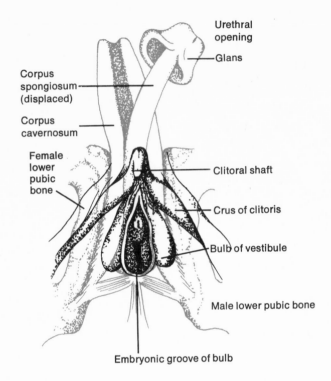

Urethral opening

Glans

Corpus spongiosum (displaced)

Corpus cavernosum

Female lower pubic bone

Clitoral shaft

Crus of clitoris

Bulb of vestibule

Male lower pubic bone

Embryonic groove of bulb

Figure VII. **Superimposition of sexual structures of female over those of male, showing greater diameter of female pelvis with greater room for expansion of cryptic structures.**

Third, as in men, the crura in women become too tendinous to expand extensively; hence most of the distension
filling up the outlet area is accomplished by the two bulbs
(Fig. VI).

Fourth, although called the bulbs of the vestibule (i.e.,
vulva) to correspond to the bulb of the penis, the bulbs are
part of the corpus spongiosum. That structure in women
has become highly modified in order to bring about the reduction in the size of the clitoral shaft. The spongiosum lost
most of its sheath; and the erectile tissue became a tangled
mass of coiled blood vessels conveying blood to and from
the bulbs to the clitoral shaft. These vessels were given the
name of the *commissure of the bulbs* (Fig. VI) back in the
days when it was thought that the clitoris was only a rudimentary penis with little or no functioning and only a few
noncongested vessels could be seen (on dissection) bridging
the distance between the bulbs and clitoral shaft. Actually,
during sexual arousal the commissure becomes very distended, a part of the total vasocongestion of the area.

Fifth, the two bulbs in women are the same as the single
bulb in men. In the female embryo the bulbs remain separated by the persistence of the vaginal canal. Each bulb is
pressed closely against the sidewalls of the lower one third
of the vagina just above the level of its orifice (Fig. VII).

Sixth, the labia minora have evolved in two ways which,
in the last analysis, permit a woman both to have an orgasm
and to conceive a baby. First, the parts of the labia that hang
down around the vaginal orifice easily developed a high
vascularity—being dependent, like the feet and ankles, they
readily become engorged; and their blood supply comes directly from that of the bulbs. Thus their marked vasocongestion permits them to add the extra length to the vaginal
canal during intercourse. Because of this connection with the
vagina, they have become especially responsive to sexual
stimulation, which means that they must have evolved many

of the special nerve endings which convey the sensation of sexual excitement. This arrangement is a potent force in directing the penis to the vaginal opening rather than elsewhere. Second, in both male and female embryos, the front portion of the labial folds connect with the skin over the penile-clitoral tubercle (Fig. VIII). This skin becomes the prepuce (in women it is called the clitoral hood). In the female this connection between labia and prepuce is maintained, thereby ensuring that the clitoral shaft will be stimulated during intercourse by the labial-preputial mechanism activated by the thrusting.

The explication of this penile-labial-preputial action, in which the labia are inducing pregnancy at one end all the while they are inducing an orgasm at the other end, is unquestionably the single most important of the many important contributions of Masters and Johnson. It has seemed to me, however, that considerable misunderstanding still prevails (seven years after the first Masters and Johnson report). The most frequent misunderstanding comes with the assertion that Masters and Johnson proved that there is no such thing as the vaginal orgasm. This is quite true (I have often worded it that way myself), *but only* if you are talking in the context of the old Freudian clitoral-vaginal theory and the superiority of the vaginal orgasm over the clitoral orgasm as a measure of maturity. Dismissing that theory now, one must think and talk in terms of a clitorally produced or a vaginally produced orgasm (or both, or a breast-produced, a thought-produced, or a whatever-produced orgasm). Physiologically all orgasms are the same.

Masters and Johnson also discovered a fact shocking to some that a clitorally induced orgasm by automanipulation can be more intense than a vaginal orgasm during intercourse. (This should not be surprising, since women must depend on the man's sexual abilities much more than vice versa; and both men and women are all too frequently still tied up in Victorian knots—knots which largely disappear

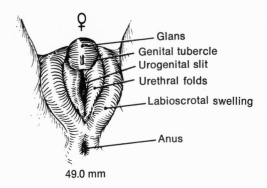

49.0 mm

Figure VIII. Female external genitalia, 49 mm. embryo, c. 7 weeks. Reproduced from illustration by Spaulding (58), as adapted by J. J. Van Wyk. In *Textbook of Endocrinology*, 3rd ed., by R. W. Williams, Philadelphia: Saunders, 1961. Reproduced by courtesy of Carnegie Institution of Washington.

when we are alone.) However, to assume that these new facts argue for the superiority of masturbation, as some have done, is sheer idiocy. Repeated masturbation is a very lonely business. I cannot imagine a single human being, short of those most disturbed or isolated from his fellows, who would prefer masturbation, however intense the orgasms, over the sharing warmth of sexual relations, however mild the orgasms, with a loved one.

Finally, the fact that the vascularity of the female pelvis is greater than that of the male deserves comment. In men most of the erectile chambers are within the sheath of the cavernous bodies (some additional distension is achieved by the pelvic venous plexi, especially around the prostate and the rectum). In women, however, sheaths of the cavernous bodies are not so strong. The blood vessels of the bulbs continue up alongside the vagina and the uterus, making this one of the most vascularized areas in the body (Fig. IX). Moreover, in men the accessory muscles producing the orgasm converge and anchor in the area behind the bulb (the *perineal body*); in women they converge both in the perineal body and also directly on the plexi of the lower one third of the vagina as well as on the bulbs. The synchronous contractions of these muscles force the blood out of the distended vessels, thus creating the orgasm. Figure X depicts the distended vascular system during intromission of an erect penis. It is quite clear from these illustrations, especially Figure X, why the length of the erect penis plays no significant role in increasing sexual excitement or orgasmic intensity in women, whereas the width of the penis is shown to be extremely important for these purposes. Not only does a widened penis create more tension on the distended bulbs, but it presses the corpus spongiosum (the commissure) against the pelvic bone (Fig. X), so that blood flow to and from the bulbs and the clitoral shaft is blocked, thereby increasing the pressure in both organs.

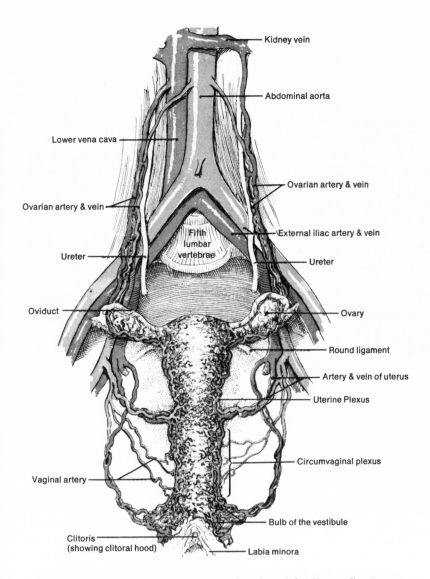

Figure IX. The blood vessels of the female pelvis. From *Gray's Anatomy of the Human Body,* 28th ed., edited by Dr. Charles M. Goss, Philadelphia: Lea & Febiger, p. 718.

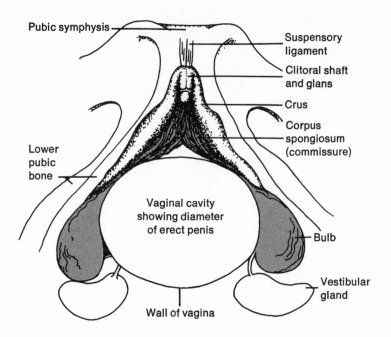

Figure X. **Distension of the clitoral system around the erect penis. Muscles, crura, and bulbs not shown.** (This illustration was published in 1949, long before Masters and Johnson's work; hence, retraction of the clitoral shaft such as would have occurred at this stage of engorgement is not depicted.) Redrawn from *Human Sex Anatomy,* 2nd ed., by Robert Latou Dickinson, Copyright 1949, Baltimore: The Williams & Wilkins Company.

It would be easy to conjecture from these anatomical observations that the orgasms would be more intense in women than in men. Such conjecturing is dangerous business, however, if only because so many immeasurable psychological factors enter the picture and because no one can really feel exactly what another may feel, let alone judge the relative degrees of pain or pleasure. I am reminded of the fate of Tiresias, the mythological prophet of the ancient Greeks, who was given the opportunity to live on earth for a time both as a man and then as a woman. The myth relates how Zeus and Hera, in one of their interminable marital bouts, argued over whether men or women have the greater sexual pleasure. With a wisdom far beyond that bourne of time and place, Zeus maintained that women have the greater pleasure. Hera, the original militant women's libber, indignantly proclaimed that everyone knows this distinction goes to the male. The couple agreed to consult Tiresias, the only person who had truly experienced both ways of being. Tiresias spoke his truth: it was more pleasurable as a woman. Whereupon Hera, furious at being deprived of the time-honored reason for resenting men, turned against Tiresias and put out his eyes—for seeing too much too wisely?

GLOSSARY

adnexa (ad nek′suh) Appendages; parts accessory to the main organ or structure. **—adnexa uteri:** uterine appendages; the fallopian tubes and ovaries. (*See also* fallopian tubes.)

adrenal gland (uh dree′nal) A ductless gland resting on the upper pole of the kidney. It is via the pituitary-adrenal-ovarian (or testes) axis that outside stimuli induce sex-hormone secretion and sexual arousal.

anastomose (uh nas′toe moze′) To open interconnecting branches, natural or surgically made, between blood vessels or other tubular structures. In the pelvic blood vessels, anastomosing permits arterial blood to flow directly into the veins, thereby mitigating the oxygen deprivation which would otherwise occur during sexual arousal as the pelvic structure becomes engorged with blood.

androgen (an′dro jen) The general term for all agents, especially testosterone, that stimulate male development in the embryo and, at puberty, stimulate the activity of the male sexual organs, which they maintain in a healthy condition.

anestrus (an′es′trus) The period in all mammals except humans of female sexual quiescence between mating seasons. (A similar period of sexual inactivity occurs in the males of most species, but it has no special name.)

anlage, pl. **anlagen** (ahn′lah guh, anh′lah gun) [Ger.] Primordium; a structure in the embryo from which an adult structure will develop.

anthropology Branch of science that treats man in all his relations.
—**cultural anthropology:** the study of men's relationships with
each other, their social customs and institutions. —**physical anthropology:** the study of the physical characteristics of man that
delineate the races of man and their evolutionary relationships.

areola, pl. **areolae** (uhree'oluh, -lee) A general term for any small
area, specifically any ringlike, pigmented area on the skin.
—**areola mammae:** the circular, pigmented area surrounding the
nipple.

atresia (uhtree'zeeah) Imperforate state; congenital absence or
pathological closure of a normal opening, tube, passage, or cavity. —**vaginal atresia:** congenital absence of the vagina.

Barr Chromosome Test (M. L. Barr, Canadian physician and geneticist) Test which allows sure sex determination from any body
cell, adult or embryo, as well as easy diagnosis of sex anomalies
due to absent or multiple sex chromosomes. When any cell (except ova) from any woman divides, one of the two sex chromosomes (XX) becomes condensed, absorbs stain and darkens,
clings to the nuclear membrane, and lags behind the other chromosomes in activity. This so-called crumpled chromosome (or
Barr body) becomes partially inactivated, and it will pass this
condensing ability to the daughter cells. In men (Xy sex chromosome complement) the small y, controlling maleness, also condenses, but then becomes too small to be seen. The reasons for
this phenomenon are not yet clear. In the Barr Chromosome Test,
cells scraped from inside the cheek are usually utilized; one Barr
body means a female, no Barr body means a male.

bisexuality A confusing word. —Popularly: the condition of one
able to have sex with a male or female. In psychiatry: the condition of an individual with normal sexual anatomy but the mind
and emotions of the opposite sex. In biology: condition of hermaphroditism, i.e., having sexual organs of both sexes. In botany:
said of a species producing separate sexes.

carpopedal spasms (car'po pee'dul) A spasm of the muscles of the
foot (more rarely of the wrist) in which the foot is held extended
with the toes pulled in; it occurs with calcium deficiency, tetany,
overbreathing, and prolonged physical activity (Popular term:
Charley-horse, said to derive from a horse named Charley at
Chattanooga baseball park noted for his lameness.)

cervicitis (ser'vih sigh'tis) Inflammation of the cervix.

cervix (ser'viks) The neck itself i.e., cervical vertebrae) and the neck of several organs. Here the cervix refers to the neck of the uterus which protrudes down into the vagina.

chronic passive congestion   Abnormal amount of blood in the vessels of any part of the body due to increased influx and/or inadequate drainage. In women this condition is caused by enlarged varicose veins of the pelvis; it is the usual by-product of two or more pregnancies and, to a lesser extent, of frequent prolonged sexual stimulation. Vessel relaxation may then render adequate expulsion of blood during orgasms impossible or completely prevent orgasms. This, in turn, increases circulatory stagnation, enhancing the varicosities. If severe, the pelvic congestion contributes to many disorders and may block venous return from the legs. This places increased strain on the heart. In this condition, all the external genitalia become swollen, waterlogged, and purple; this condition is very uncomfortable, and the sensation of unrelieved sexual tension readily passes into cramps and pain.

clitoridectomy (klit'oruhdect'omee), from **clitoris** (klit'oris)   Excision or amputation of the clitoris. An operation rarely done today (except in radical pelvic surgery for cancer); it was a standard procedure during the Victorian period as the cure for excessive masturbation or nymphomania, and has a long history in many ancient and preliterate cultures.

cloaca (clo ay'kuh)   In the embryos of all vertebrates (and many invertebrates) the beginning intestines, kidneys, sex ducts and yolk sacs all empty into a common chamber with a single orifice; hence the term "cloaca," which means sewer. The more primitive animals keep the cloaca unchanged; in more advanced ones, a partition soon grows down separating the rectum from the chamber receiving urine and sexual products. (The yolk-sac duct withers when yolk is exhausted.) In the most advanced animals, including man, a second partition forms separating the urine and genital chambers. In congenital anomalies, a persistent cloaca may be found, in which intestines, bladder, and sex ducts merge internally and have a single outlet.

coaptation (co'ap tay'shun)   The joining or fitting together of two surfaces. At rest the opposite sides of the vagina are fitted (or pressed) together eliminating the vaginal cavity.

coition, coitus (koish'un, ko'itus)   Sexual union, copulation.

colposcope (kol'poscope')   Instrument for examining the interior of the vagina; it magnifies the cells of the vagina and cervix for direct observation.

cornification (corn'ificay'shun) The process whereby the cells of the skin, hair and the vaginal wall become charged with keratin, a substance which kills the cells and transforms them into the hard, protective masses we call hooves, calluses, etc. In the vagina, at the middle of every menstrual month, estrogen acts to transform the soft tender cells into the tougher stratified, cornified cells. The two possibilities one can imagine for this occurrence are (1) it renders the vagina stronger for the more frequent sexual acts during the last half of the menstrual cycle; (2) it is an evolutionary hangover since the creation of a vaginal cavity occurred by cornification of the area and then the sloughing away of the cornified cells.

corpora, sing. **corpus,** any body or mass. The main part of an organ or structure.

corpus luteum (cor'pus loo'tee um') The yellow zone surrounding the egg and containing hormones which stimulate the uterus to prepare for pregnancy. Immature eggs lie imbedded in follicles in the outer layer of the ovary. Each month one egg matures; its follicle grows larger and moves nearer the surface where it can be seen with the naked eye. At ovulation the follicle ruptures; the egg escapes into the fallopian tube. The burst follicle becomes vascular and even larger and is surrounded by the corpus luteum, which contains the same pigment as in egg yolks. Its cells secrete the hormone progesterone, which then stimulates the uterus to prepare for pregnancy. If pregnancy ensues, the corpus luteum continues to grow, and secretes progesterone and other hormones throughout the next nine months. If not, the corpus luteum regresses to a tiny white scar on the surface of the ovary.

crura, sing. **crus** (kroo'ruh, kroos) Structures resembling a leg or a root. —**crura of the corpora cavernosum:** the diverging proximal ends of the main portion of the penis which attach to the lower pelvic bone. —**crura of the clitoris:** the homologous structure in the female.

cyclicity (sigh clis'ih tee) A recent medical usage meaning the general state of specified cycles or rhythms; means approximately the same as cycling; here refers to the estrus or the menstrual cycles. (*See also* estrus.)

cytology (sigh tol'ojee) —**1:** The anatomy, physiology, pathology, and chemistry of the cells; the study of cells; —**2:** In common medical usage: the state of any given cells at the moment examined (e.g., "The cytology was negative").

decidua (dee cid'yoo uh) That part of the lining of the uterus that builds up each month and becomes part of the placenta if a fertilized egg is implanted; if the egg is unfertilized, the shed decidua is the menstrual flow.

detumescence (dee'too mess'ens) Subsidence of a swelling. (*See also* tumescence.)

differentiation The process of becoming different from the original state. —**embryonic differentiation:** process in which the undifferentiated cells change into specialized more advanced or adult forms. —**primary sexual differentiation:** the cells of the primordial genital ridge in early embryos change into either ovary or testes. —**secondary sexual differentiation:** when primary sexual differentiation has occurred, the estrogen or testosterone produced initiates the process in which the cells of the genital ducts and other secondary sexual structures change into the male or female forms of them.

dimorphism (dye mor'fizim) Existing in two forms. —**sexual dimorphism:** the existence of different male and female forms.

ectoderm (ek'toe derm') In all early embryos, the rapidly dividing cells arrange themselves in three hollow cylinders within each other. The inner cylinder of cells, the endoderm, will become the intestinal tract and blood vessels; the middle cylinder, the mesoderm, becomes the connective and reproductive tract tissue; the outer layer, the ectoderm, becomes the skin and the nervous system.

dorsal The back, upper, or posterior surface of any part.

edema, adj. **edematous** (ih dee'muh, ih dem'a tus) A perceptible accumulation of excessive clear watery fluid in tissues. At one time commonly called dropsy. The commonest form is sexual edema of the female, i.e., the accumulation of fluid in the pelvic tissues, which passes through the vaginal wall to form the vaginal transudate or lubrication. (*See also* transudate.)

embryogenesis (em bree'o gen'uh sis) Embryonic development from the end of the second week after fertilization to the end of the eighth week when the conceptus is called a fetus.

encephalization (en cef'a lie zay'shun) Corticalization; in the progressive advance of higher forms of animal life, encephalization refers to the migration of brain functions from lower or subcortical centers to the cerebral cortex.

endocrinology (en'do crin ol'o gee) Science that studies the endocrine, or ductless, glands.

endoderm; entoderm (en'do derm) The innermost of the three primary germ cell layers of the early embryo. (*See also* ectoderm.)

episiotomy (eh pee'see ot'o mee) Surgical incision of the opening of the vagina during childbirth when laceration or tears seem imminent. Obstetricians advise routine episiotomies during the first delivery and often use them for all deliveries.

epithelial cells (ep'i thee'lee al) Thin, avascular layer of cells covering all free surfaces, including skin, mucous membranes, and the glands and other structures within these parts.

erectile bodies Here refers to the substance of the penis and clitoris composed of large blood sinuses and a mechanism that can decrease blood outflow. When this gating mechanism occurs, the sinuses become enlarged with blood, the organ enlarges and hardens, and the muscles surrounding the erectile bodies are stretched, triggering an erection.

estrogen Female steroid hormones that produce estrus, ovulation, and the growth of female secondary sexual characteristics. Actually estrogen, not estrogens, is the correct usage since we now know there are many closely related estrogenic hormones in animals, plants, and many made synthetically (one called estradiol is the chief hormone made by the human ovary), and the term "estrogen" covers them all.

estrus (ess'trus) (Brit. oestrus) Heat; that portion of the estrus or sexual cycle of female animals when they will accept the male. (The scientific name of the family of insects containing the gadfly or botfly is Oestridae.)

ethology Term in ethics and philosophy recently adopted by animal psychologists. In word usage now obsolete, the word meant the science of character and ethics; and before that, the portrayal of character by mimicry. Now means the study of animal character and the relationship of animals to their environments.

exogenous (ek soj'eh nus) Originating or produced outside; exogenous hormones are those made outside the subject's body and administered as medication or for experimental purposes.

extravasation (ex tra va say'shun) —1: The act of blood, lymph, or blood serum escaping from a vessel into the tissues. —2: The material in tissues that has escaped from a blood or lymph vessel; an exudate (e.g., edema fluid is an extravasation).

fallopian tubes (fa low'pee en) [from Gabriele Fallopio, Italian anatomist of 16th century who first discerned their function] Oviducts: the tubes leading down from each ovary to the main body of the uterus. The ovarian end cups around and over the ovary, and has a flared fringed end which opens into the intestinal cavity (called its fimbriated end). We inherited these tubes from our ancestors, and they may have functioned well as egg-catchers and egg-conveyors for animals on four legs, but are somewhat less than adequate for our upright position. Not infrequently eggs miss the opening and escape into the peritoneal cavity causing trouble. The folded lining of the tube makes it easy for fertilized eggs to implant in them instead of the uterus and an unattended tubal pregnancy will rupture, causing a serious emergency.

false pelvis (also **large pelvis**, or **pelvis major**) The upper, large, flared portion of the pelvis, whereas the true pelvis (small pelvis, pelvis minor) is the lower narrowed portion of the pelvic bone. A wide false pelvis may give the false impression that a woman should deliver a baby with ease. The lower outlet of the true pelvis forms the narrowest portion of the birth canal through which the baby's head must pass undamaged.

fascia (fash'yah) **—deep fascia:** The sheets of fibrous connective tissue, devoid of fat, that enclose each muscle or muscle group, form nerve and vessel sheaths, and become specialized at joints to form the ligaments or strengthen them. **—superficial fascia:** The more loosely organized fascia that envelops the body beneath the skin; it contains fat, blood vessels, and nerves.

fetalization (fee'tal i zay'shun) Evolutionary theory of: (1) the persistence of certain fetal characteristics of the ancestors into adult life; thus the human adult is supposed to resemble an ape fetus more than the ape adult. The theory has no adequate proof; (2) the prolongation of fetal life into early infancy producing later ages of maturation in humans.

fixation As used by Freud, denotes psychopathic state in which psychic energy originally attached to components of the infantile stage is not abandoned, or sublimated in favor of more mature behavior.

fornices (for'ni ces), sing. **fornix** Arched structures. The vaginal fornices are made by the recess at the top or vault of the vagina surrounding the cervix of the uterus.

follicular phase (fol lik'yoo lar) Denotes the first half of the estrus cycle when the immature ovum that has lain inert in a nest of cells since it formed in early embryonic life begins to mature. The surrounding cells also stir, multiply and form a mature nest from which the egg is extruded at the middle of the cycle.

fourchette (foor shet') The small fold of membrane that connects the labia minora at the posterior part of the vaginal opening.

fulminating Running a speedy course with rapid worsening.

gametes, heterogametic or **homogametic** (ga'meets, het'ur o guh mee'tik, ho'mo guh mee'tik) —**gametes:** the collective term for matured ova or sperm that have halved their chromosome number and are ready to unite to form a new individual. In many species, including man, the immature ovum has the XX pattern (so each gamete contains one X); the female has two similar sex chromosomes and is homogametic. The male's two chromosomes are different: half of his gametes are X; half are y; he is heterogametic. In many other species (especially birds and reptiles) the pattern is reversed: the female has the heterogametic Xy and the male has the homogametic XX.

genetic sex Sex has several determinants, even such things as diet and climate in the lower animals. In man, sex is basically determined by the result of the union of one sex chromosome from the mother with one from the father. Usually subsequent forces only reinforce the genetic sex. However, the genetic sex may encounter reversing forces that lead to more or less ambiguity in the adult. Hence the genetic sex, the anatomic sex, and the sex of rearing may be different, leading to more or less pronounced sexual pathology or psychopathology.

genetic variability In all species, every gene is more or less locked into a larger gene complex. Any one trait may thus be closed to evolutionary change if changing it would require a damaging or fatal change in the whole complex. Such major changes occur, if at all, only by the slow accumulation of minute variations over millions of years. Other traits are not tied to vital genetic complexes and are more open to change. These give the species or an individual its genetic variability and produce the individual differences within a species.

glans (glanz), pl. **glandes** (glan'deez) Conical vascular body which forms the tip of the penis or clitoris. —**glandar,** adj.: coined by author as shortened term for the adjectives glandarious or glandiform.

gonads (go'nads) Collective term for ovaries and testes.

hermaphroditism (hur maf'ro dye tiz'um) A congenital disorder in which both male and female generative organs exist in the same individual. —**true hermaphroditism:** ovaries and testes as well as secondary sexual characteristics exist in the same person. —**pseudo hermaphroditism** or **false hermaphroditism:** the outward secondary characteristics are both male and female but the individual has either ovaries or testes, not both.

heterotypic (het'er o tip'ik) Pertaining to or characteristic of a type other than that normally encountered or expected.

homologue, adj. **homologous** (hom'uh log', ho'mol' o gus) Any organ or part of one animal that corresponds in some way to an organ or part of another animal, especially in origin, position, or structure (but not function). Thus, the wing of a bird and bat are the homologue of the arm of a man.

homotypic (ho'mo tip'ik) Pertaining to an organ or part with the same structure or function as another, especially one on the opposite side of the body; corresponding to the second of two paired organs.

17-hydroprogesterone (hy'dro pro ges'ter own) Hormone closely related to progesterone.

hyperhormonalization (hy'per hor mo'nal eye zay'shun) The large supply of many hormones to the body at a rapid rate. Hyperhormonalization is most often associated with the rapid supply of many hormones that occurs at puberty or with pregnancy.

hypertrophy (hy per'tro fee) Overgrowth; general increase in bulk of an organ or part not due to tumor formation.

hyperventilation (hy'per vent'i lay'shun) Overbreathing producing increased pulmonary ventilation beyond that needed to maintain blood gases within normal range. Hyperventilation causes the blowing off of carbon dioxide and increases oxygen supply to the red blood cells and from there to the brain. If severe, dizziness, spasms, and convulsions may occur.

hysterectomy (his'ter ek'to mee) Removal of the uterus.

inductor An agent that evokes an effect. **—embryonic inductor substances:** in embryonic growth, an organizer or inductor substance in one cell or several cells induces differentiation of adjacent cells. **—inductor theory of sexual differentiation:** inductor substances from the primordial germ cells induce the differentiation of fetal structures along male or female lines. These would be either testicular or ovarian inductor substances.

infraprimates (in'fra pry'mates) All species of mammals below the primates in levels of intellect and manual dexterity.

inguinal canal (in'gwi nal) Canal running from an opening in the lower margins of the peritoneal cavity to the scrotal sac in males and to the labia majora in females. In males the spermatic cord runs up from the testes and through the canal into the penis. In females the canal is normally a solid cord. Especially in men the peritoneal opening of the inguinal canal may remain enlarged from fetal life so that an inguinal hernia may result.

Insectivora (in'sec tiv'or ah) An order of mammals whose chief food is insects; it includes moles, shrews, and anteaters.

labia, sing. **labium** (lay'bee ah, lay'bee um) Lips. —**labia majora:** (muh jor'uh) outer of the two folds that form the flanks of the vulva, arises just below the mons pubis and is covered with pubic hair. —**labia minora:** (mee nor'uh) inner folds that flank the vulva; covered with highly vascular mucous membranes, wrinkled, and hairless.

lumen (loo'men) The space in the interior of a tubular structure, such as an artery or the intestine; the hole in the tube.

luteal phase (loo'tee al') The last half of the estrus or menstrual cycle between ovulation (about 14th day in humans) and the onset of the next menses, during which the follicle from which the egg was extruded turns into the corpus luteum and secretes progesterone.

mesoderm (mess'o derm) The earliest embryo is made up of three layers; the middle layer is the mesoderm and from it will come the vascular and reproductive systems.

mons (monz) An eminence. —**mons pubis,** syn. **mons area:** The eminence at the front of the body over the pubic symphysis, the bone underlying the pubic area. Covered with hair and is a sensitive erotic zone.

morphogenesis, adj. **morphogenetic** (mor'fo jen'e sis, mor'fojanet' ik) The differentiation of cells and tissues in the early embryo which results in establishing the form and structure of the various parts of the body. Also used to denote similar differentiation, which occurs in the regeneration of a part of the body that has been damaged or cut off.

mucification (mew'si fi cay'shun) The softer, non-cornified state of the vaginal lining during the first half of the menstrual cycle. Associated with a change of the vaginal wall cells into a taller form. These columnar cells can be stimulated into the production of mucus. (*See also* cornification.)

mucoid (mew'koid) Resembling mucus, the fluid secreted by all mucous membranes.

mucosa (mew ko'za) Same as mucous membrane.

multipara (mul tip'a rah), adj. **multiparous** A woman who has had two or more pregnancies resulting in viable offspring. Multigravida means a woman who has been pregnant two or more times. —**multiparity:** the condition of having had two or more children.

nidation (nye day'shun) Nest-building. Medical term: the embedding of the early embryo in the uterine mucosa.

nonparous (non pare'us) (*See* parity.)

nullipara (nul lip'er uh) (*See* parity.)

occlusion (uh kloo'zhun) The act of closing or state of being closed.

ontogeny (on tahj'e nee) The embryonic developmental growth of the individual as distinguished from phylogeny, the evolutionary development of the species.

oviparity (oh'vi pair'i tee), adj. **oviparous** Egg-laying; denoting those animals, such as birds, whose ova are developed outside the body.

ovulation (ov'yoo lay'shun), adj. **ovulatory** The escape of the ovum from its follicle on the surface of the ovary.

palaeontology The study of extinct plants and animals, usually confined to extinct animals.

papillary (pap'i lar'ee) Relating to, resembling, or provided with papillae, any small nipple-like projection or process. —**papillary rash:** one in which the reddened areas protrude upward like tiny nipples.

parity, adj. **parous** The state of a woman as regards the fact of having borne children. Medical shorthand: parity followed by a number equals number of children woman has borne (e.g., parity 5 = woman who has borne 5 children). —**decipara:** woman who has borne ten children. —**nulliparity:** state of having had no children. —**primiparity:** state of having had one child.

pathognomonic (path'og no mon'ik) Characteristic or indicative of a disease; denoting especially one or more symptoms typical of a specific disease.

patulous (pat'yoolus) Patent, lying freely open.

perineum (pe ri'nee'um) The area between the thighs extending from the tip of the coccyx behind to the pubic bone in front, and bounded above by the pelvic diaphragm. (See illustration, pp. 59, 63 of perineum body and perineum membrane.

pH Initials for potential of hydrogen, a measure of the acidity or alkalinity of a solution. A pH of 7 is neutral, one of more than 7 is alkaline and one of less than 7 is acid.

phylogeny, adj. **phylogenetic** (fye lodge'eh nee, fye'lo jeh neh'tik) Evolutionary development of a species; the racial history of any organ or structure. —**phylogenetic series:** Examples of the successive evolutionary changes of a species or part through specified points in time.

Pleistocene epoch (plice'teh seen') Geological term for the most recent epoch of the Cenozoic era. This epoch lasted about 2 million years, and included the last four great glaciations. It ended about 10,000 years ago.

plexi (plek'see), sing. **plexus** Networks. Interjoining of nerves, veins, arteries, or lymphatics.

polyandry (pol'ee an'dree) That form of polygamy in which one woman has two or more husbands at the same time, **polygyny** (pol lij'a nee) being the term for the form of polygamy in which a man has two or more wives at one time. Note: The word "polygamy" is correctly used to describe the practice by either female or male of having more than one spouse simultaneously. Since polygamy most often took the form of polygyny, colloquial usage incorrectly restricted the word "polygamy" to polygynous marriages.

postpartum (post'par'tum) Pertaining to, or occurring during, the period following childbirth.

prepartum (pree'par'tum) Pertaining to or occurring during the period before delivery, any time during pregnancy.

prepuce (pree'pyoos) Foreskin; fold of skin covering head of penis or clitoris. —**preputial-glandar mechanism** (pree'pu'shal glan'dar) A phrase coined by the author to denote the physiological activity, first discovered by Masters and Johnson, whereby the clitoris is indirectly stimulated by the penis during intercourse. The thrusting movement of the penis in the vagina pulls on the labia minora which, via their extension around the clitoris (clitoral hood or prepuce) is then pulled back and forth over the erect, retracted clitoris.

primatology (pry'muh tol'o gee) The study of the primate, the highest order of mammals including man, apes, monkeys and lemurs.

primitive streak The first visible cluster of cells which indicates the head-tail axis of the embryo.

primordial germ cells (pry mor'dee al) In the earliest embryo, certain cells stand out by virtue of being large and darker staining. They contain much DNA which itself can be traced back to patches of DNA in the fertilized egg. These cells, the primordial germ cells, are located at first in different areas in different species; some at different areas along the outside margins of the embryo, others completely outside the embryo in the surrounding nutritional membranes. They move like amoebae and migrate either directly or indirectly through blood vessels to the cell clump (the genital ridge) which will form the structural elements of the ovaries or testes. Here they settle down in the middle of the gonad if they are male and around its margins if they are female; and the gonad then differentiates to match. Many primordial germ cells do not reach their goal; they die off.

progesterone (pro ges'ter own) The hormone secreted by the corpus luteum of the ovary which stimulates the uterus to prepare for pregnancy, regulates the periodicity of the sexual cycle, inhibits the uterine contractions, relaxes pelvic ligaments and stimulates the mammary glands.

progestins (pro ges'tins) The generic term for all the related chemicals having progesterone-like effects, including both those released by the corpus luteum and placenta and those made synthetically.

psychobiology The science of personality formation and function. A term used variously to denote (1) the total person, mind and body, (2) the understanding of the development of mental illness and its treatment as taught by Adolph Meyer of Johns Hopkins University.

psychopathology The specific symptoms, with their underlying mental and emotional dysfunctioning and the history of their development, which characterize psychiatric illness.

pudendum (pew den'dum) External genital organ, especially the vulva. —**pudendal overhang:** position of clitoris vis-à-vis the vulva when a woman is on her back.

reflex ovulation In most animals the egg will mature and escape from its follicular nest only when the follicle is stimulated by intercourse (or by the changes occurrent with sexual excitement).

reflex stretch mechanism A phrase denoting the fact that a muscle is stimulated to contract when it has been passively stretched to a certain degree; the stretching then reflexively stimulates the muscle to contract. There are special nerve endings in these kinds of muscles that are responsive only to stretching.

refractory Strongly opposed; not readily yielding to a prescription; obstinate; not susceptible to change. —**refractory period:** A resting phase in activity marked by the inability of a structure to function.

reproductive isolation The isolation of a species so that inbreeding will occur. Reproductive isolation is most frequently produced in nature because of geographical obstacles (rivers, oceans, mountains, etc.), but a host of other restraints to the free-flow of genes also operates.

resorb (ree sorb') To reabsorb; to absorb what has been excreted or formed to be excreted. Usually such material passes into the bloodstream and is broken down in the liver and excreted via the kidneys.

retraction —1: A drawing back; a shrinking. —2: Action of a muscle that draws a part backward.

retroflexion, retroflection Backward bending, as of the uterus when its body is bent back toward the vertebrae, so that it forms an angle with the cervix.

Rodentia (ro den'sha) An order of mammals which possess one or two pairs of long incisor teeth adapted for gnawing; contains mice, rats, rabbits, guinea pigs, beavers, etc.

rudimentary Imperfectly developed. In the embryo a structure in its first recognizable form.

ruga, pl. **rugae** (roo'guh, roo'jee) A fold, ridge, crease, or wrinkle. The mucous membrane of vagina, in the relaxed state, collapses into a number of transverse ridges or rugae.

selective pressure In evolution a trait is said to be under strong selective pressure when conditions are such that some change is decidedly advantageous to survival and there are no obstacles to the free flow of the responsible gene(s) through the gene pool. The selective pressure may also be nil, weak, or moderate.

serous (seer'us) Relating to, containing, or producing serum or a substance having a similar watery consistency, e.g., serous membranes, serous glands.

sex reversal—1: In experimental embryology, a condition created by experimental means in which the established sex is reversed during embryological development. —2: State achieved by surgery in hermaphrodites so that the sex is changed from male to female, or vice versa.

sinusoid (sign'u soid') —1: Resembling a sinus. —2: A blood channel in certain organs which, when enlarged with anastomosing and with valves that prevent or impede outflow, forms the vascular plexi characteristic of the clitoral bulbs and erectile tissue of the penis. (*See also* anastomosing.)

soma The body (as distinct from the mind, intellect or emotions).

supine (soo pine') Lying on the back. (The female supine position in coitus is the most commonly used.)

suprapubic skin (soo'pra pew'bik) The area of skin between the umbilicus and the pubic bone. The area is characterized by the growth upward of pubic hair in men and none in women; it is highly sensitive to erotic stimulation.

symphysis (sim′fi sis) A binding of bones, so that there is no movable joint. —**pubic symphysis:** the joining at the two pelvic bones at the front of the body with strong fibrous tissue which, nonetheless, responds to pregnancy hormones, so that it relaxes to increase the size of the birth canal.

testosterone (tess tos′ter own′) The male sex hormone obtained in crystalline form from the tissue of the testes of bulls or made synthetically. (*See also* androgen.)

therapsid (ther ap′sid) An order of extinct reptiles which were warm-blooded and are believed to be the connecting link in evolutionary progress from the cold-blooded reptiles to the warm-blooded mammals.

transudation (tran′soo day′shun) The passage of a fluid through a membrane. Differs from osmosis in that all the salts and other substances are carried with the fluid through the membrane. The passage results from a difference in hydrostatic pressure.

tubercle (too′bur cal) A circumscribed, rounded, solid elevation on the skin or surface of any organ. The penile-clitoral or genital tubercle is the rounded protuberance in the early embryo which will become the penis in males and the clitoris in females.

tumescence (too mess′ens) A swelling.

urethral sphincter (yoo ree′thral sphink′ter) Muscle fibres surrounding that section of the urinary tube (urethra) leading out from the bladder, which controls urination. This section of the urethra passes through the prostate in men and lies near the external urinary opening in women.

urogenital sinus (yoor′o jen′i tul) In the very early embryo, the lower intestine widens into the cloaca which also receives the kidney and gonadal ducts. A septum soon grows down dividing the cloaca into the rear rectal chamber and the forward urogenital sinus. The lower portion of the urogenital sinus exteriorizes as a groove running to the base of the penile-clitoral tubercle and is flanked by lubicle folds. In males, the folds encircle the urogenital sinus to form the urinary tube and main body of the penis. In females, the folds remain open and the lower urogenital sinus becomes the vestibule, receiving the urethra and vaginal opening and the clitoris at the anterior end. (*See also* cloaca.)

vaginality (vaj′i nal′i tee) The erroneous concept, developed in psychoanalysis, that the capacity for orgasms in females had to be transferred from the clitoris to the vagina during the process of normal maturation; i.e., normal women were said to have developed a mature vaginality.

varicosities (vair′i cos′i tees) Dilated portions of veins; such veins are swollen, knotted and tortuous. The circulation distal to the swollen veins is impaired.

vascularity (vas′kyoo lair′i tee) The quality of being vascular or provided with arteries and veins.

vas deferens (vas deaf′er enz′) The tube that carries the semen and sperm away from the testes; the spermatic cord.

vasotension (vas′o ten′shun) The tone or tension within a blood vessel.

vasocongestion (vas′o kun jes′chun) State of an organ or part into which blood can flow but from which outflow is impeded.

vasodilatation (vas′o dill uh tay′shun) Dilation of blood vessels. **—capillary vasodilatation:** the dilation of the small arteries leading from the arterial to the venous systems. These vessels are equipped with special nerve endings making them a key factor in the control of the peripheral circulation and blood pressure. (Capillary vasodilatation is the reason why we can blush so quickly and capillary constriction why we can turn pale so quickly.)

ventrodorsal Indicating a position in coitus in which the male's abdomen is against the female's back; also called female knee-chest position or rear entering. A similar position is used in anal intercourse.

vestigial (ves tih′jee′al) A remnant or trace of something formerly present. Synonymous with rudimentary but also often used to connote a structure from embryonic life which has left only the barest trace in the adult. Usually discernible only with the microscope.

viscera (vis′sir uh), sing. **viscus** The organs enclosed in the four great body spaces: the head, chest, abdomen, and pelvis. The term usually refers to those organs within the abdominal cavity.

viviparity (vee′vi pair′i tee) Condition of bringing forth living young, as distinguished from oviparity.

vulva, adj. **vulvar** (vul′vuh) The external sexual organs of the female.

vulvectomy (vul vec′toe mee) The surgical operation which removes all the external genitalia of a woman plus all the blood vessels and lymphatics possible. Indicated only in cancer of the area.

witch's milk Old lay term for the milk that is sometimes secreted by the breasts of male or female newborn infants. Such milk comes from the excessive amounts of female sex hormones that have passed to the baby from the mother during pregnancy. The milk disappears in a few hours after the baby is cut off from the mother's circulation.

SOURCES

1. Aaronson, L. R. "Hormones and Reproductive Behavior: Some Phylogenetic Considerations," in *Comparative Endocrinology*, edited by A. Gorbman. New York: John Wiley & Sons, 1959.
2. Bachofen, J. J. *Das Mutterrecht* (1861). Basel: Benno Schwabe, 1948.
3. Barr, M. L. "Cytologic Test of Chromosomal Sex," in *Progress in Gynecology*. New York: Grune & Stratton, 1957, Vol. 3, pp. 131–41.
4. ———, "Chromosomal Abnormalities," in *First Inter-American Conference on Congenital Defects*. Philadelphia: Lippincott, 1963, pp. 70–88.
5. Beach, F. A. *Hormones and Behavior*. New York: Harper & Row, 1948.
6. Bieber, E. L. "Critique of the Libido Theory." *Journal of the American Psychoanalytic Association*, Vol. 18 (1958), pp. 52–65.
7. Bliss, E. L., ed., *Roots of Behavior*. New York: Harper & Row, 1962.
8. Bonaparte, M. *Female Sexuality*. New York: International Universities Press, 1953.
9. Burns, R. D. "Role of Hormones in the Differentiation of Sex," in *Sex and Internal Secretions*, edited by W. C. Young. 2 vols. Baltimore: Williams & Wilkins, 3rd ed., 1961, Vol. 1, pp. 1173–1239.

10. Brash, J. C., ed., *Cunningham's Textbook of Anatomy*. London: Oxford University Press, 9th ed., 1953.
11. Davies, J. *Human Developmental Anatomy*. New York: Ronald Press, 1963.
12. Devereux, G. "The Significance of the External Female Genitalia and of Female Orgasm for the Male." *Journal of the American Psychoanalytic Association,* Vol. 6, 1958, pp. 278–86.
13. Dickinson, R. L. *Atlas of Human Sex Anatomy*. Baltimore: Williams & Wilkins, 1949.
14. Erkin, W. "Social Behavior and the Evolution of Man's Mental Faculties," in *Culture and the Evolution of Man,* edited by M. F. A. Montagu. London: Oxford University Press, 1962.
15. Ford, C. S., and Beach, F. A. *Patterns of Sexual Behavior*. New York: Harper, 1951.
16. Freud, S. "Three Essays on the Theory of Sexuality (1905) *Standard Edition*. London: Hogarth Press, Vol. 7, 1953, pp. 125–245.
17. ———, "Beyond the Pleasure Principle" (1920) *Standard Edition*. London: Hogarth Press, Vol. 18, 1955, pp. 3–64.
18. Gorbman, A., and Gern, H. A. *A Textbook of Comparative Endocrinology*. New York: John Wiley & Sons, 1962.
19. Guhl, A. M. "Gonadal Hormones and Social Behavior in Infrahuman Vertebrates," in *Sex and Internal Secretions,* edited by W. C. Younge. 2 vols. Baltimore: Williams & Wilkins, 3rd ed., 1961, Vol. I, pp. 1240–67.
20. Hamilton, W. J., Boyd, J. D., and Mossman, H. W. *Human Embryology*. Baltimore: Williams & Wilkins, 1962.
21. Hampson, J. L., and Hampson, J. G. "The Ontogenesis of Sexual Behavior in Man," in *Sex and Internal Secretions,* edited by W. C. Younge. 2 vols. Baltimore: Williams & Wilkins, 3rd ed., 1961, Vol. 2, pp. 1407–32.
22. Hawkes, J., and Woolley, L. *History of Mankind,* Vol. I, *Prehistory and the Beginnings of Civilization*. New York: Harper & Row, 1963.
23. Heiman, M. "Sexual Response in Women: A Correlation of Physiological Findings with Psychoanalytic Concepts." *Journal of the American Psychoanalytic Association,* Vol. 11, 1963, pp. 360–87.
24. Hill, W. C. O. *Primates, Comparative Anatomy and Taxonomy,* 5 vols. Edinburgh: University Press, 1953, 1955, 1957, 1960, 1963.

25. ———, Personal communication.
26. Hisaw, F. L., and F. L., Jr. "Action of Estrogen and Progesterone on the Reproductive Tract of Lower Primates," in *Sex and Internal Secretions,* edited by W. C. Younge. 2 vols. Baltimore: Williams & Wilkins, 3rd ed., 1961, Vol. 1, pp. 556–89.
27. Jones, H. W., and Wilkins, L. "The Genital Anomaly Associated with Prenatal Exposure to Progesterone." *Fertility and Sterility,* Vol. 11, 1960, pp. 148–56.
28. Jost, A. "Problems of Fetal Endocrinology: the Gonadal and Hypophyseal Hormones," in *Recent Progress in Hormone Research,* edited by G. Pincus. New York: Academic Press, 1953, Vol. 8, p. 379.
29. Kardiner, A., Karush, A., and Ovesey, L. A. "Methodological Study of Freudian Theory." *Journal of Nervous and Mental Disease,* Vol. 129, 1956, pp. 11–19, 133–43, 207–21, 341–56.
30. Kinsey, A. C., Pomeroy, W. B., Martin, C. E., and Gebhard, P. H. *Sexual Behavior of the Human Female.* Philadelphia: Saunders, 1948.
31. *Ibid.,* 1953.
32. Kubie, L. S. "Influence of Symbolic Processes on the Role of Instincts in Human Behavior." *Psychosomatic Medicine,* Vol. 18, 1956, pp. 189–208.
33. Lehrman, D. S. "Hormonal Regulation of Parental Behavior in Birds and Infrahuman Mammals," in *Sex and Internal Secretions,* edited by W. C. Younge. 2 vols. Baltimore: Williams & Wilkins, 3rd ed., 1961, Vol. 2, pp. 1268–1382.
34. ———, "Interaction of Hormonal and Experiential Influences on Development of Behavior," in *Roots of Behavior,* edited by E. L. Bliss. New York: Harper, 1962, pp. 142–56.
35. Lichtenstein, H. "Identity and Sexuality: A Study of Their Interrelationship in Man." *Journal of the American Psychoanalytic Association,* Vol. 9, 1961, pp. 179–260.
36. Lillie, F. *Sex and Internal Secretions.* Baltimore: Williams & Wilkins, 1932.
37. Lorand, S. "Contributions to the Problem of Vaginal Orgasm." *International Journal of Psychoanalysis,* Vol. 20, 1939, pp. 432–8.
38. Lundberg, F., and Farnham, M. *Modern Women: The Lost Sex.* New York: Harper, 1947.
39. Marmor, J. "Some Considerations Concerning Orgasm in the Female." *Psychosomatic Medicine,* Vol. 16, 1954, pp. 240–5.

40. Maslow, A. H., Rand, H., and Newman, S. "Some Parallels between Sexual and Dominance Behavior of Infrahuman Primates and the Fantasies of Patients in Psychotherapy." *Journal of Nervous and Mental Disease,* Vol. 131, 1960, pp. 202–12.

41. Masters, W. H. Personal communication.

42. ————. "The Sexual Response Cycle of the Human Female." *Western Journal of Surgery, Obstetrics, and Gynecology,* Vol. 68, 1960, pp. 57–72.

43. ————, and Grady, M. H. "Estrogen-Androgen Substitution Therapy in the Aged Female: II. Clinical Responses." *Obstetrics and Gynecology,* Vol. 2, 1953, pp. 139–41.

44. ————, and Johnson, V. "The Physiology of the Vaginal Reproductive Function." *Western Journal of Surgery, Obstetrics and Gynecology,* Vol. 69, 1961, pp. 105–120.

45. ————, ————, "The Artificial Vagina: Anatomic, Physiologic, Psychosexual Function." *Western Journal of Surgery, Obstetrics and Gynecology,* Vol. 69, 1961, pp. 192–212.

46. ————, ————, "The Sexual Response Cycle of the Human Female. III. The Clitoris: Anatomic and Clinical Considerations." *Western Journal of Surgery, Obstetrics and Gynecology,* Vol. 70, 1962, pp. 248–57.

47. ————, ————, "The Sexual Response Cycle of the Human Male." *Western Journal of Surgery, Obstetrics and Gynecology,* Vol. 71, 1963, pp. 85–95.

48. ————, ————, "Orgasm, Anatomy of the Female," in *Encyclopedia of Sexual Behavior,* edited by A. Ellis and A. Abarbanel. New York: Hawthorn Books, 1961, Vol. 2, p. 702. 792 ?

49. Mayr, E. *Animal Species and Evolution.* Cambridge: Harvard University Press, 1963.

50. Money, J. "Sex Hormones and Other Variables in Human Eroticism," in *Sex and Internal Secretions,* edited by W. C. Younge. 2 vols. Baltimore: Williams & Wilkins, 3rd ed., 1961, Vol. 2, pp. 1383–1400.

51. Moore, B. E. "Panel Report: Frigidity in Women." *Journal of the American Psychoanalytic Association,* Vol. 9, 1961, pp. 571–84.

52. Ostow, M. "The Erotic Instincts: A Contribution to the Study of Instincts." *International Journal of Psychoanalysis,* Vol. 38, 1957, pp. 305–27.

53. Rado, S. "A Critical Examination of the Concept of Bisexu-

ality." *Psychosomatic Medicine,* Vol. 2, 1940, pp. 459–67.

54. ————, "An Adaptational View of Sexual Behavior," in *Psychoanalysis of Behavior.* New York: Grune & Stratton, 1956, p. 201.

55. Ryan, K. J. "Synthesis of Hormones in the Ovary," in *The Ovary* (International Academy of Pathology monograph), edited by H. G. Grady and D. E. Smith. Baltimore: Williams and Wilkins, 1963.

56. Schimel, J. L. "The Psychopathology of Egalitarianism in Sexual Relations." *Psychiatry,* Vol. 25, 1962, pp. 182–86.

57. Shettles, L. B. "Ovulation: Normal and Abnormal," in *The Ovary* (International Academy of Pathology monograph), edited by H. G. Grady and D. E. Smith. Baltimore: Williams & Wilkins, 1963.

58. Spaulding, M. H. "The Development of the External Genitalia in the Human Embryo." *Carnegie Institute Washington Contributions in Embryology.* Vol. 13, 1921, p. 69.

59. Taylor, E. S. *Essentials of Gynecology.* 2nd ed. Philadelphia: Lea & Febiger, 1962.

60. Van Wyk, J. J. "Pathogenesis of Sexual Anomalies," in *The Ovary* (International Academy of Pathology monograph), edited by H. G. Grady and D. E. Smith. Baltimore: Williams & Wilkins, 1963.

61. Wiesman, A. I. *Spermatozoa and Sterility.* New York: Hoeber, 1941.

62. Wiesner, B. P. "The Postnatal Development of the Genital Organs of the Albino Rat, with Discussions of a New Theory of Sexual Differentiation." *Journal of Obstetrics and Gynecology of the British Empire,* Vol. 41, 1934, p. 867; Vol. 42, 1934, p. 8.

63. Wilkins, L., Jones, H. W., Holman, G. H., and Stempfel, R. S. "Masculinization of the Female Fetus Associated with Administration of Oral and Intramuscular Progestins during Gestation: Nonadrenal Female Pseudohermaphroditism." *Journal of Clinical Endocrinology,* Vol. 18, 1958, pp. 559–585.

64. Wilson, J. G. "Genitourinary Defects," in *First Inter-American Conference on Congenital Defects.* Philadelphia: Lippincott, 1963, pp. 106–18.

65. Witschi, E. "Embryology of the Ovary." *The Ovary* (International Academy of Pathology monograph), edited by H. G.

Grady and D. E. Smith. Baltimore: Williams & Wilkins, 1963.

66. Young, W. C. "The Hormones and Mating Behavior," in *Sex and Internal Secretions,* edited by W. C. Younge. 2 vols. Baltimore: Williams & Wilkins, 3rd ed., 1961, Vol. 2, pp. 1173–1239.

About the Author

MARY JANE SHERFEY was born in Brazil, Indiana. She received her B.A. from the University of Indiana, where she studied with the late Alfred Kinsey, and her M.D. from the University of Indiana Medical School. She took her general internship in Vancouver, Canada, where she planned to remain as a resident in pediatrics. Instead, she chose psychiatry and became a resident in psychiatry at the Payne Whitney Clinic of the University of Cornell Medical School in New York where she trained under the outstanding psychiatric educator, Professor Oskar Diethelm.

In 1955 she was appointed Assistant Professor of Psychiatry at the Cornell Medical School. Shortly thereafter, she left this appointment for private practice and the freedom to undertake further research in the physiology of the sexual response in human females and among the higher primates.

Dr. Sherfey is currently a practicing psychiatrist in New York City and is at work on Volume II of *The Nature and Evolution of Female Sexuality.*